TO DISCLOSE OR NOT TO DISCLOSE, THAT IS THE QUESTION!

SELF-REVELATION'S IMPACT ON THE DISCLOSING THERAPIST

DR GENEVIEVE MARAIS

First Published 2024 by Dr Genevieve Marias

ISBN 978-1-0369-0662-7 (Print)
ISBN 978-1-0369-0663-4 (eBook)

Cover Design and Interior Formatting by Gregg Davies Media (Pty)Ltd
www.greggdavies.com

Acknowledgments

The author is immensely grateful to the courageous participants who engaged in the study because it is their efforts that have allowed this book to be manifest. I would like to extend my gratitude to Oli, who worked with me in bringing this book into being.

Preface

Genevieve Marais is a practising Counselling Psychologist and Integrative Psychotherapist. She is a Chartered member with the British Psychological Society and is also registered with the United Kingdom Council for Psychotherapy. She has a keen interest in mind-body connection and body wisdom and has trained in Energy Psychotherapy.

This book endeavours to draw attention to the subject of therapist self-disclosure, with a specific focus on the impact self-disclosure has on the disclosing therapist. Literature and research appear to focus heavily on the use of therapist self-disclosure in relation to its impact on the client and this is understandable as we, as therapists, are there to be of beneficence for the client within the therapeutic relationship. This book recognises the humanness and fallibility incumbent in all human beings, and therapists are not exempt from this. Holding in mind the two-way dialogue and the notion of two subjectivities meeting within the intersubjective space, it felt vital to give focus to the personal experience self-disclosure may have on the disclosing therapist.

I dedicate this book to Steven who has always supported me in my therapeutic journey and encouraged me to step into the arena to be seen. I make a further dedication to Alistair who motivated me to write this book.

Declaration

The information in this book is derived from my doctoral thesis, which also produced a follow-up article on the subject matter of therapist self-disclosure and was co-authored with my research supervisor. As a result, parts of the texts may resemble, replicate and/or overlap with my published original doctoral thesis and the subsequent journal article and hence have been reproduced with the consent of the editors.

Contents

Chapter 1
An Introduction to Self-Disclosure

Therapist self-disclosure is a multi-faceted concept encompassing the therapist's attitudes, emotional states and perceptions of the therapeutic encounter. This concept involves the dynamic interplay of transference and countertransference within the therapeutic space, shaped by both implicit and explicit responses and embodied experiences. Acknowledging these dynamics underscores the importance of the interpersonal processes within the inter-subjective exchange (Stolorow, Atwood, & Brandchaft, 1987). While therapist self-disclosure is an acutely relevant topic, it remains a contentious one in counselling psychology and psychotherapy, with many ethical debates and divergent opinions arising over its role in therapy. Although its use in individual therapy is widely recognised, it is applied with caution and with limited frequency (Brown & Walker, 1990; Farber, 2006; Goldfried, Burckell, & Eubanks-Carter, 2003; Lane & Hull, 1990; Mahalik, Van Ormer, & Simi, 2000).

Clinical literature indicates that the nature and extent of therapist self-disclosure varies across theoretical orientations (Maroda, 1991; Yalom, 2002). Research has primarily focused on the impact of therapist self-disclosure on client personal growth and well-being. However, therapists' personal experience of self-disclosure remains under-explored, as is the impact it may have on them. Given the reciprocal nature of disclosure, it is posited that therapist self-disclosure, while intended to benefit clients, may also affect therapists. This book aims to explore therapist self-disclosure with a view to examining its impact on the personal experience of the disclosing therapist.

It specifically focuses on how therapists use their own experiences and vulnerabilities to aid clients' healing and how they manage the personal impacts of their self-disclosures. It is hoped that it may contribute to professionalism, practice, training, ethics, and self-care by exploring this complex phenomenon within counselling psychology and psychotherapy, a field that incorporates various psychotherapeutic models to honour individual uniqueness within the therapeutic relationship (Lapworth, Sills, & Fish, 2001), and thereby provide relevant insights for a broad range of counselling psychology and psychotherapy practices.

My interest in this topic stems from experiences I have had within personal therapy and clinical work, having encountered both beneficial and detrimental instances of therapist self-disclosure, leading to therapy transformation or rupture. These experiences have highlighted the ambiguities of self-disclosure and fuelled my curiosity into its impact on the therapeutic relationship. Ever since I was a trainee, I have been fascinated by how therapists grapple with self-disclosure's practicalities and ethical implications, especially given its 'taboo' status in clinical practice. Throughout my work in personal therapy, my clinical practice and supervision, I have observed varying levels of therapist self-disclosure, and this has further piqued my interest.

Self-disclosure remains a controversial topic within counselling psychology and psychotherapy owing to its potentially positive and negative effects on client healing. Experience and skill are crucial in managing the embodied states and dynamics it evokes, such as projective identification and parallel processes (Maroda, 1991; Clarkson, 1995). Maintaining empathic curiosity about self-disclosure's impact on both clients and therapists is essential for ethical and professional practice as well as self-care. As a client, when engaged in my own personal therapy, my experience of self-disclosure's varied impacts has given me an appreciation of its complexities and shaped my cautious approach to its use in therapy.

This book aims to address a neglected area of therapist self-disclosure - the potential impact on the disclosing therapist. Although extensive research has explored therapist self-disclosure's impact on clients (Audet & Everall, 2003; Farber, 2006; Gibson, 2012; Knox, Hess, Peterson, & Hill, 1997; Knox & Hill, 2003), there is a lack of coherent definitions or frameworks to understand it comprehensively. The duality inherent in the therapist-client relationship necessitates examining therapist self-disclosure from the therapist's perspective.

By focusing on the personal impact and experience of therapist self-disclosure, the insights provided in this book aim to enhance therapists' self-reflexivity and self-awareness, in the hope they will improve ethical practice as well as client and therapist care. It is also hoped that a book focused on this subject matter from the perspective of the disclosing therapist will encourage practitioners to discuss and address self-revelation in training, practice and supervision, potentially bridging the gap between theory, practice and ethics (Audet, 2011). In addition, by exploring how therapists decide to disclose, I hope the book will help develop guidance for managing self-disclosure's complexities.

In conclusion, this book aims to bridge a knowledge gap by exploring therapist self-disclosure's personal impact and experience on the disclosing therapist. It seeks to challenge prevailing attitudes, provide clinically relevant insights, and promote ongoing dialogue and further exploration within the professional and clinical spheres. By enhancing understanding and self-reflexivity, as well as encouraging continuing discourse, this book seeks to support ethical and effective therapeutic practice.

Chapter 2
Self-disclosure across Theoretical Orientations - a Brief Historical Overview

Empirical studies acknowledge the longstanding debate regarding therapist self-disclosure and its role in counselling psychology and psychotherapy. Farber (2006) argues that therapist self-disclosure within individual adult therapy has received significant attention. Regarding client outcomes, self-disclosure's complexity is demonstrated in relation to its sub-types, varying dimensions, content, effects, and frequency of use (Farber, 2006). However, there seems to be a gap in empirical research in this area, with the impact on the therapist appearing to have been neglected. This book aims to provide a contextual appreciation of the understanding and meaning therapists attribute to their 'lived experience' (Smith et al., 2009) of self-disclosure.

Historical Context

Researching the historical context has highlighted the powerful influence therapists' theoretical orientations have on this subject. Theoretical orientation and training heavily influence therapists' decisions to engage in self-disclosure. The differing schools of thought are somewhat binary in their approach to this subject, with one side perceiving therapist self-disclosure as therapeutic and the other side seeing it as harmful. Thus, acknowledging its position within the historical context is crucial.

Psychoanalytic and Psychodynamic Perspectives

Early theorists within the psychoanalytic and psychodynamic fields consider therapist self-disclosure as harmful to the therapist-client relationship, as it blurs boundaries and shifted attention away from the client (Farber, 2006). Freud (1912) initially advocates a 'blank screen' approach to avoid contamination of the therapeutic space. However, Freud himself experiences challenges regarding 'the blank screen', thus adaptations within his own psychoanalytic dyads were inevitable in this respect. Later, he comes to recognise that both self-disclosure and non-disclosure had their benefits and pitfalls. Consequently, Freud (1912) acknowledges the dilemma this subject presented by noting 'self-disclosure demonstrably undermines our attempts to conduct analysis [and] refusing to reveal ourselves demonstrably undermines our attempt to conduct analysis' (Freud, 1912, cited in Greenberg, 1995, p.195). Later theorists such as Ferenczi (1926) and Khan (1986) begin to actively experiment with self-disclosure, arguing that therapists should see themselves as active participants in therapy.

Contemporary psychoanalysis, which advocates a more relational and intersubjective perspective (Stolorow et al, 1987), recognises the significance of selective and judicious countertransference self-disclosure. The psychoanalytic perspective asserts that therapist self-disclosure should be cautiously applied in a considered manner and introduced only when it is of benefit to the client (Lane & Hull, 1990).

Behavioural-Cognitive Perspective

Behavioural-Cognitive therapists are more reticent on the issue of self-disclosure but acknowledge its benefits for building the therapeutic relationship and supporting client self-awareness (Goldfried, Burckell, & Eubanks-Carter, 2003). They recognise that therapist self-disclosure can help clients manage and decrease symptoms of distress, strengthen the working alliance and create more positive perceptions of the therapist. However, early-stage disclosures by the therapist are discouraged owing to their potential to negatively impact the therapist-client relationship. Risks include alienating the client or shifting the focus away from the client and on to the therapist (Goldfried et al., 2003).

Humanistic and Existential Perspectives

Humanistic therapists hold a more open view of therapist self-disclosure, aligning with Rogers' (1951) core conditions of empathy, congruence and unconditional positive regard. Both Rogers (1951) and Jourard (1971) emphasise the importance of self-disclosure in establishing a therapeutic connection, seeing its value in boosting rapport, trust, intimacy, self-awareness, and ultimately facilitating change. Humanistic and existential perspectives recognise the two-way interaction between therapist and client, which goes beyond transference and countertransference. Existential perspectives argue that therapists should be open about their coping strategies and beliefs regarding existential concerns, enabling clients to internalise and integrate these processes (Jourard, 1971; Yalom, 2002). They recognise this openness as fostering authenticity and believe it potentially creates opportunities for 'I Thou' moments (Buber, 1958) where two subjectivities experience a real, authentic meeting.

Feminist Perspective

Feminist therapists support self-disclosure for its potential to reduce power imbalances in the therapist-client relationship and empower clients (Mahalik, Van Ormer, & Simi, 2000). Therapist self-disclosure encourages clients to view their difficulties with empathy and compassion, aiding in their empowerment and emancipation from struggles (Greenspan, 1986; Brown & Walker, 1990). Feminist therapists emphasise that self-disclosure should benefit the client and not serve the therapist's needs or self-gratification.

Summary of the Historical Context

The theoretical frameworks discussed, despite their distinct focuses, agree that therapist self-disclosure is an inescapable and necessary part of therapeutic work. Zur and Lazarus (2002) state that while some warn against self-disclosure due to potential boundary crossing, others recognise its therapeutic value. All perspectives emphasise caution and ethical considerations, ensuring self-disclosure primarily benefits the client and does not shift focus onto the therapist.

Empirical Studies on Therapist Self-Disclosure

The empirical literature on therapist self-disclosure highlights its multi-faceted nature, noting its different types, content, timing, and impact on the therapeutic process. Farber (2006) identifies different sub-types of self-disclosure: those of facts, feelings, and insights. Each type serves different therapeutic purposes and must be used judiciously to avoid shifting focus from the client to the therapist. Research by Hill et al (1988) and Knox et al (1997) underscores the importance of timing in self- disclosure. Early revelations can hinder the development of the therapeutic alliance, while revelations later in therapy can strengthen the relationship and model coping strategies for clients. Additionally, Goldfried et al. (2003) finds that self-disclosure can enhance the therapist-client bond and support clients in symptom management and cognitive restructuring. Farber (2006) also places emphasis on the content of self-disclosure, noting that revelations about therapeutic progress, the therapist's feelings towards the client, and personal experiences relevant to the client's issues are most beneficial. However, disclosures unrelated to the client's experience can be distracting and counterproductive.

Despite the extensive research on the impact of therapist self-disclosure on clients, the effects on therapists remain under-explored. Studies by Audet and Everall (2003) and Gibson (2012) suggest that therapist self-disclosure can enhance therapist authenticity and job satisfaction, but they also raise concerns about therapist vulnerability and boundary management. While substantial research exists on the effects of therapist self-disclosure on clients, there is a notable gap regarding its impact on therapists. The existing literature focuses primarily on client outcomes, with limited attention to how therapist self-disclosure affects therapists' emotional, psychological and professional experiences. This book aims to address this gap by exploring the personal experiences and impacts of therapist self-disclosure on the disclosing therapist, contributing to a more comprehensive understanding of this complex phenomenon.

Conclusion

Therapist self-disclosure is a nuanced and complex aspect of therapeutic practice, with significant implications for both clients and therapists. The historical and empirical literature highlights diverse perspectives on its use, benefits and risks. Consequently, this literature review underscores the need for further research into the impact of self-disclosure on therapists, and aims to enhance ethical practice, therapist wellbeing and, ultimately, client outcomes.

Chapter 3
The Myth of Neutrality within Self-Disclosure and the Essence of Human Subjectivity

Greenberg (1995, p.195), dispels the possibility of neutrality within the therapist-client relationship, asserting that 'everything that a therapist does or does not do reveals something of the therapist to the perceptive patient'. This, in alignment with the view of Jourard (1971) that through self-disclosure, individuals come to know themselves and others; the very notion of self-disclosure highlights the essentially relational nature of human interaction. Self-disclosure is integral to human experience from birth (Bowlby, 1998; Stern, 1998) through the life cycle (Fairbairn, 2010) and possibly even pre-birth, as suggested by neuroscientific investigations (Schore, 2005; Siegel, 1999). These early experiences shape one's sense of self and interactions with others, encompassing pre-verbal, non-verbal, and verbal exchanges.

Empirical evidence and literature reviews (Freud, 1912; Goldfried et al, 2003; Jourard, 1971; Lane & Hull, 1990; Mahalik et al., 2000; Rogers, 1951; Audet & Everall, 2003; Farber, 2006; Gibson, 2012; Knox et al, 1997; Knox & Hill, 2003) indicate that neutrality is an illusion in human encounters, whereas self-disclosure remains constant. Given the relational dynamics at play, it is essential to explore the impact of therapist self-disclosure on the disclosing therapist within this two-way interpersonal process, as opposed to a linear perspective that may feel oppositional to two-person psychology (Stark, 2000) and the intersubjective meeting (Stolorow et al, 1987).

Definition of Therapist Self-Disclosure

Given the complexity of this phenomenon, it is crucial to adopt a 'loosely held definition' of therapist self-disclosure. Broadly speaking, therapist self-disclosure can be defined as the process by which the therapist reveals personal information about themselves (feelings, thoughts, experiences) to their clients for therapeutic benefit (Audet & Everall, 2003; Knox & Hill, 2003). However, because of the complexities of human interaction, multiple types of therapist self-disclosure exist.

Owing to this multifaceted nature, arriving at a definitive framework is challenging. The term 'therapist self-disclosure' can be misinterpreted to suggest one specific behaviour, but empirical research reveals significant variability in its interpretation across therapists, researchers, theoretical orientations, and therapeutic disciplines (Pizer, 1993; Audet & Everall, 2003; Farber, 2006; Gibson, 2012; Knox et al., 1997; Knox & Hill, 2003). For example, Pizer (1993) concentrates on the importance of the therapist's reasons for engaging in self-disclosure, which are often governed by affective processes and countertransference, or owing to unavoidable circumstances, such as illness or pregnancy.

Operational Definitions

Therapist self-disclosure can be verbal and non-verbal, intentional and unintentional (Knox et al, 1997). Greenberg (1995) emphasises the point that therapists reveal aspects of themselves consciously and unconsciously through their interactions with clients. Consequently, all forms of therapist self-disclosure hold significance for the therapist-client relationship and warrant further investigation.

Non-Immediate Intentional Therapist Self-Disclosure

Non-immediate therapist self-disclosure involves 'verbalised personal revelations made by the counsellor to the client' (Watkins, 1990, p. 478). Simon (1990) defines it as being when therapists consciously communicate private information about themselves to their clients. For, example, by sharing personal details or experiences. This type of disclosure validates client experiences and includes sharing feelings, experiences, coping strategies, and responses that support the therapeutic process (Farber, 2006).

Immediate Self-Involving, Unintentional, Accidental, and Countertransference Self-Disclosure

Immediate self-disclosure can be defined as the therapist's expressions of their feelings about the client, the therapeutic relationship, or moments that occur during the session (Gibson, 2012). These disclosures, also known as self-involving, immediacy or countertransference revelations, reveal how therapists are impacted by their clients (Farber, 2006). This type of disclosure might involve the therapist's emotional responses (for example: 'I feel angry when I hear how you are treated by your partner') or highlight the intersubjective dynamics between therapist and client (for example: 'I wonder what is happening between us right now because it feels like you are disconnecting').

The Complexity of Therapist Self-Disclosure

The complexity of therapist self-disclosure can be seen in the myriad ways it manifests, which include verbal, non-verbal, deliberate, and accidental disclosures (Farber, 2006).

Disclosures can be direct or indirect (Gibson, 2012). Research distinguishes several subtypes, such as positive or negative feelings, thoughts, reactions to client reactions, and acknowledgment of mistakes (Audet, 2011; Farber, 2006; Hoffman-Graff, 1977). Although defining boundaries is challenging, experts identify two primary types of therapist self-disclosure: immediate and non-immediate (Audet, 2011; Farber, 2006; Knox et al, 1997).

The Advantages and Disadvantages of Therapist Self-Disclosure

Conflicted perspectives and ambivalence prevail regarding therapist self-disclosure. While it can be a powerful tool for therapeutic transformation, it also poses risks. Therapist self-disclosure enhances awareness of countertransference reactions and encourages therapist self-reflection (Maroda, 1991). However, it is important to note that disclosures can lead to role reversal, shifting the therapeutic focus from the client to the therapist, and potentially causing harm if the self-disclosures are poorly timed or excessive (Zahm, 1998; Audet, 2011). Pointing to the elements of risk-taking and vulnerability it involves, Jourard (1971) emphasises the innate humanness of self-disclosure. While it can develop and strengthen human relationships, leading to potential 'I-Thou' moments (Buber, 1958), Farber (2006) warns of the balance between helpful sharing and the dangers of over-disclosure. Although he acknowledges that self-disclosure is inevitable, he concedes that defining this phenomenon remains problematic, as 'disclosures involve negotiating an appropriate balance between the helpfulness of sharing a part of ourselves with another and the inappropriateness or even danger of overdoing it, or perhaps sharing too much too soon' (Farber, 2006, p.1).

Casement (2019) alerts us to the risk of therapists unwittingly revealing aspects of their own thinking that may cause ruptures to the analytic process - occasions when the therapist's interpretation of a given moment and the client's interpretation of the therapist's thinking reveals to the client what has been occupying their therapist's mind. This may alarm clients, causing them to become hyper-vigilant, distrusting of their therapist, and to behave differently to feel 'safe' in their presence (Casement, 2019). Renik (1995), meanwhile, points to the advantages of self-disclosure - asserting that change and the transformation of wounds in the service of healing for self-and-other cannot materialise without it, or, more specifically, intentional and explicit therapist self-disclosures.

Bridges (2001) concedes that intentional therapist self-disclosure (sharing personal/private information, opinions) can benefit the client, deepening the therapeutic relationship so that unconscious client material can surface and be worked with therapeutically. Sullivan (1954) encourages therapists to consider using their self-disclosure as a means of countertransference response, thus providing clients with valuable insight into themselves. Disclosure facilitates rapport, trust, understanding (Wells, 1994), and encourages reciprocal self-disclosure by the client (Saffron & Muran, 2000).

Thus, Sullivan (1954) regards the idea of therapist neutrality as an impossibility within the therapist-client relationship. As a result of this, the therapist assumes the role of 'participant observer' (Sullivan, 1954) within the interpersonal realm, in which both subjectivities reflect their experiences, meaning-making and interpretation of their respective 'lived experience' (Smith et al, 2009). Interpersonal neuroscience research highlights the relational component and right brain-to-right brain interaction (Schore, 2005), indicating that self-disclosure can aid the active rewiring of the brain, supporting greater integration and self-awareness (Siegel, 1999).

Yalom (2002, p.83) states that 'there is every real reason to reveal yourself to the patient and no good reason for concealment'. In my opinion, this position appears to lack necessary boundaries and could be considered as being neglectful of the possibility of harm to the client (and by implication, the personal and professional self of the therapist). Wachtel (2008) takes an opposing view, warning of the dangers introduced by such an unbridled stance by highlighting the 'misperception that to work relationally means to disclose relentlessly' (Wachtel, 2008, p. 245). Casement (2019) provides a very modern counter-position regarding self-disclosure, in relation to the historic blank-screen notion of a therapist's neutrality. He alerts us to the potential dangers of working in a 'detached way' and how this can adversely impact the client and the therapeutic relationship, suggesting that adhering to an 'obsessive neutrality' may significantly compromise the analytic process.

Self-disclosure can be considered a doubled-edged sword in respect of therapeutic benefit and harm. Given this, it is legitimate to wonder how therapists feel about themselves after making a disclosure. Though therapist self-disclosure helps clients see their therapists as human, imperfect and fallible, these moments also have the potential for clients to view their therapists with suspicion regarding their motives or to aggrandise them (Rowan & Jacobs, 2002). 'The patient's idealisation [of their therapist] can lead to even greater idealisation, because such honesty can make the therapist into an even more admired figure' (Rowan & Jacobs, 2002, p.66).

Therapist self-disclosure is observed to be a powerful tool that can potentially be therapeutically transformative or create ruptures in the therapeutic relationship. Spinelli (2002) argues that self-disclosure needs to serve as a therapeutically appropriate tool for client benefit and touches on its potential benefit for the therapist (2005). Spinelli (2005, p.148) argues that 'the we-focused realm of encounter is characterised by its immediacy [in which therapist and client experience], "us" being in relation with one another'. Consequently, it is when both client and therapist operate from the inter-relational realm that therapist self-disclosure may prove beneficial to the client (and, by implication, the therapist). In this sense, it allows the client and therapist opportunities to be open to a different/alternate understanding of their interaction with self-and-self and self-and-other.

Casement (2019) uses the term 'self-revelation' as an expression of self-disclosure and explores this notion through countertransference, writing that when therapists examine their countertransference responses involving self-revelations, they may be faced with looking at the parts of themselves they often disown. To illustrate this, he uses the example of a situation in which he unconsciously worked to hold a rigidly neutral stance and distance from a female client whom he found attractive (Casement, 2019). His realisation of this led him to offer his client a reparative experience by owning his mistakes. In this way, his client may have benefited from exploring and understanding her issue from a different perspective, which was equally valuable and therapeutically productive (Casement, 2019).

Negative outcomes of therapist self-disclosure have been associated with frequency of use, repetitive and lengthy disclosures, poor attunement or incongruence with the client's issues (Audet, 2011; Gibson, 2012). In these instances, clients potentially feel criticised or emotionally injured, and left with a sense that they (client) are wrong, rather than holding the view that their position is different and equally valuable (Zahm, 1998). These negative outcomes may also lead to ruptures and hinder progress or continuation in therapy (Safran & Muran, 2000). Further consequences involve role reversal - shifting the therapeutic focus from client to therapist - leaving clients feeling obliged to respond in ways that they perceive their therapist might need, hence adopting the care-taking role (Zahm, 1998). In some instances, therapist self-disclosure may leave clients feeling burdened, inhibited in what they feel they can share and distrusting of their therapists' intentions (Audet, 2011).

Self-disclosure can also make problematic the process of distinguishing between transference and objective realities involving the analytic relationship (Casement, 2019). Nevertheless, Casement (2019, p.78) continues to hold a both/and position, stating that sometimes 'it helps the patient to know enough of the analyst's reality to be able to recognise when it is transference that is predominating in the analytic relationship and when it is not'.

The therapist's non-defensive honesty may allow clients to feel more able to use their therapist as a 'good enough' (Winnicott, 1965) 'self-object' (Kohut, 1971), when previous caregivers may have been unwilling or unavailable to meet the client's developmental needs. In this sense, self-disclosure may offer the client a different and corrective emotional experience (Alexander, 1961). In consensus with Zahm (1998), Casement (2019, p.74) also alludes to the burden that an analyst's self-disclosure may place on the client – it may leave the client feeling manipulated by their therapist's direct response or 'anxious about the analyst's ability to contain him/her, and therefore others'. Despite the ambiguous nature of this phenomenon, there is consensus among the majority of perspectives that therapist self-disclosure needs to be applied cautiously and with the therapist remaining 'attentive to the consequences' (Wachtel, 2008, p. 247).

The above viewpoints all point to the two-way process involved in the therapeutic relationship and I understand this acknowledgement to translate to therapist self-disclosure. For this reason, in therapists' accounts - bearing in mind that much of this two-way process is acknowledged - it feels important to explore the personal experience and impact of therapist self-disclosure on the disclosing therapist. Delving into therapist self-disclosure highlights the challenges and difficulties therapists face when contemplating a disclosure. Researchers recognise that therapist self-disclosure encourages client self-disclosure (Knox et al, 1997; Knox & Hill, 2003), thus acknowledging the fluidity of the co-created process (Stolorow et al, 1987).

The literature on the subject indicates that withholding disclosures may result in ruptures within the therapist-client relationship (Ehrenberg, 1995; Safran & Muran, 2000), leaving clients feeling rejected, and perceiving their therapist as aloof and impersonal (Safran & Muran, 2000). Therapists acknowledge the need to avoid or withhold self-disclosures when it may result in shifting the focus away from the client or interfere with the client's process, material, transference and blurred boundaries (Simon, 1990).

Ehrenberg (1995, p.225) argues that 'remaining silent here is as potentially problematic and as potentially toxic as any other response'. To my mind, her view is a recognition of the dangers and risks involved in therapist non-disclosure, as these moments can be experienced as withholding by a client and prove injurious to their trauma/emotional wounds. Furthermore, avoiding all therapist self-disclosure to reduce risk and harm can contaminate the therapist-client relationship, doing the client a disservice (Hanson, 2005; Zur, 2009). Orange, Atwood and Stolorow (1997, p.31) acknowledge the perplexing nature of this phenomenon by recognising that 'neither disclosures nor withholdings are neutral'.

Spinelli (2002) concedes that decisions to disclose or not to disclose should be based on therapeutic benefit for the client. Thus, disclosures need to be focused on exploring those conditions and circumstances that relate to the issues and concerns presented by the client (Spinelli, 2002). In this way, therapist self-disclosure may allow for clarification and increased awareness on the part of the client in terms of how they view and experience themselves in relation to others and the world (Spinelli, 2002).

It is my view that therapist self-disclosure should not be viewed in binary terms, as it remains an unavoidable phenomenon within the therapeutic dyad. Instead, and in agreement with Spinelli (2002), particular attention should be placed on *'when'* to disclose and when to withhold from disclosing. Although my own study [*The Impact and experience of Therapist Self-Disclosure on the Disclosing Therapist (2019)*] agrees with Spinelli's (2002) view, it also asks, in respect of this 'we-focused realm' (Spinelli, 2005, p.148), what about the personal experience and impact of therapist self-disclosure on the disclosing therapist?

Granted that therapist self-disclosure offers considerable inroads for movement, progress, transformation and positivity within the therapist-client relationship, Storr's (1990) contribution alerts us to risks involving its potential shadow side. Storr (1990) mentions an example in which, by his own admission, his 'thoughtless' and 'caught- by-surprise' response to his client's question resulted in his self-disclosure proving to be counter-therapeutic. As a result, therapy with this client ended abruptly. The client appeared to be struggling with guilt and shame regarding his sexual practices and Storr's (1990) decision to assert that he engaged in similar sexual practices proved injurious to his client. Upon reflection, Storr (1990) was able to see how his spontaneous self-disclosure had disillusioned his client and interrupted his client's phantasies about him as a therapist – hence breaking the transference.

Storr's (1990) attempt to meet his client's needs while also remaining authentic, congruent and human resulted in his self-disclosure proving emotionally injurious, disillusioning his client and dispelling his client's phantasies. Hence, Storr's (1990) 'thoughtless' confirmation to his client's question prevented his client from using his phantasies in his own way, as a means of exploring and understanding his own internal world (Casement, 2019).

This experience offers an illustration of the reasons for withholding disclosures and highlights the need to explore the client's reasons for asking their therapist personal questions (Casement, 2019). It adds weight to Freud's (1912) reasons for deterring therapists from engaging in self-disclosure. The personal impact on Storr (1990) was a sense of regret. He (Storr, 1990) had missed an opportunity to curiously and empathically explore what it would mean for his client if he did or did not masturbate, and his self-disclosure thwarted any further opportunity to explore his client's phantasies as it resulted in a rupture and the abrupt termination of therapy (Storr, 1990). This example demonstrates the delicate interplay encompassed in self-disclosure and its power to destroy the therapeutic relationship, emotionally injure the client and possibly the therapist. It also shows how, owing to their essentially human and subjective composition, therapists, just like their clients, also seek acceptance and validation (Storr, 1990). Moreover, it alerts one to the shadow side of therapist self-disclosure in which the therapist's own self-disclosure can offer the therapist an opportunity to self-indulge in their unresolved issues, emotional injuries, deficits and traumas (Storr, 1990).

The above-mentioned episode also alerts one to the relational dynamics within the therapeutic encounter. Self-disclosure can enhance or break the therapist-client relationship, but it also has the potential to take a professional relationship into the realm of friendship (Storr, 1990). Storr (1990, p. 67) argues 'the job of the therapist is to understand his patient, not obtain understanding from his patient [and therefore] psychotherapy is bound to be a one-sided relationship'. I disagree with Storr's (1990) view that psychotherapy is a one-sided relationship and instead hold the opinion that the practice of psychotherapy and counselling psychology cannot be divorced from our essentially subjective and intrinsically human composition as it is by embracing these qualities (which often involve elements of self-disclosure) that human beings, therapist and client, can work together and explore possibilities for transformation and healing. In this respect, 'psychotherapy will always remain more of an art than a science' (Storr, 1990, p.69).

Non-Disclosure Benefits

Given the potential risks of therapist self-disclosure, the decision to adopt a non-disclosing stance should also be acknowledged. Non-disclosure allows therapists to present models of boundaries and safety, supporting clients in managing relational boundaries and integrating these processes into their lives (Sweezey, 2005). It also protects therapists' personal information, as the asymmetric nature of the therapeutic relationship does not offer therapists the confidentiality and protection their clients receive (Maroda, 1991).

Conclusion

Therapist self-disclosure is a complex and multi-faceted phenomenon with significant implications for both therapists and clients. It can enhance therapeutic relationships and client outcomes but also poses risks if it is not managed judiciously. Furthermore, owning that not knowing how one's self-revelation may land with a given client in itself implies risk. Understanding the various types, benefits and disadvantages of therapist self-disclosure is essential for ethical and effective therapeutic practice. In this respect, this book encourages the need for further research into the personal experiences and impacts of therapist self-disclosure on the disclosing therapist to help provide a more comprehensive understanding of this nuanced aspect of how this phenomenon impacts the therapy.

Chapter 4
The Tensions between the Personal and Professional Roles of the Therapist

Grappling with the notion of what motivates therapists to work with and hold the tensions of their professional and personal roles in relation to self-disclosure and client reactions is complex, nuanced and intriguing. I lean towards the concept of multiple truths and multiple realities. Consequently, this leads me to suggest that however one chooses to look at, perceive, explore and understand this topic, one will always arrive only at a partial revealing of the 'truth' (Braud & Anderson, 1998) given our individual and unique standpoints and life experiences. How any individual attempts to unpack these tensions will be heavily influenced by their subjectivity, 'pre-understandings' (Gadamar, 1990) and 'givens' (Heidegger,1962). Ultimately, truth remains a mystery and therefore exists in multiple forms and at multiple levels (Braud & Anderson, 1998).

Therapists are faced with a very real and emotionally wrenching battle when they wrestle with their professional roles versus their personal roles in relation to how these aspects play out in the therapeutic dyad. It is a battle that can be summarised with these questions: does one disclose or does one hold a non-disclosing stance? What will be the impact on the client? What will be the impact on the therapist? How does one remain professional and yet honour and demonstrate authenticity and humanity? Thus, the conflict between the personal and professional selves of the therapist during therapeutic encounters with their clients requires rigorous, conscious self-reflexivity, critical awareness and constant assessing and re-assessing of moment-by-moment interaction.

There is consensus between the historical and literature reviews that therapist self-disclosure should be used only when it will be therapeutically beneficial for the client. Hence, it appears that in these moments what propels therapists to take the risk and engage in self-revealing disclosures with a given client (risking the professional and personal pieces respectively) may stem from an inherent responsibility to serve as a healing presence for them (Rowan & Jacobs, 2002). Consequently, the fundamental question must always be: *Who is it for?* Motivation, power, humanity, humility, acceptance, the shadow, and a desire to facilitate the client's healing process are all intertwined within the notion of what 'drives' therapists to disclose (Storr, 1990). Essentially, our need to disclose may be the result of our innate need to know self-and-other (Jourad, 1971), magnifying the significance of this very subjective experience. Bearing in mind the duality that exists within this co-created encounter (Stolorow et al 1987), it is imperative that therapists remain cognisant of the ethical implications and risks (for both self and other) while sharing their personal piece for their client's benefit.

In these moments, there appears to be a rapport between their personal and professional roles in correlation with the reciprocal mutual influence (Stolorow et al, 1987). Hence, these moments potentially signify a web of belonging within a universal emotional tapestry interwoven with varying degrees of experience that both therapist and client can intimately access. In this sense, it can be acknowledged that vulnerability is an important factor in self-disclosure. No therapist is ever exempt from feelings of vulnerability (Baldwin, 2000). It can be argued that the therapist's motivation to hold the tensions between their professional and personal selves resonates with their awareness of their position as wounded healers (Jung, 1993). There is a sense of the 'innate knowing' of a oneness within all things and of all things

(Braud & Anderson, 1998), hence the idea that revealing our woundedness will allow the client to access their own inner healer (Rowan & Jacobs, 2002). It can also be argued that what inspires therapists to adopt a both/and position regarding the tensions between their professional and personal roles is a need to strive towards one's deepest destiny – authenticity (Heidegger, 1962). Following on, it is noted that these personal and professional tensions translate into ethics and practice.

Taking into consideration this phenomenon alongside the above-mentioned tensions emphasises the complexities involved in this subject matter, the differing variables at play and the many levels and degrees of engagement and revelation that interweave between the therapist's personal and professional roles. Consequently, the notion of therapist neutrality (Greenberg, 1995) and the 'blank screen' (Freud, 1912) appear to be invalidated by the unquestionable and constant presence of the issue of self-disclosure in the therapist's relationship with a client. Hence, the therapist's innate desire to embrace being thrown into these moments and being with the other (Heidegger, 1962) also extends to incorporating their personal and professional selves within this process. Thus, there remains a continuous struggle between fallenness and authenticity (Heidegger, 1962).

Exploring this issue from a transpersonal perspective highlights our futile attempts as human beings (and therapists) to keep control of and maintain a grasp on reality (Braud & Anderson, 1998). In this sense, the transpersonal offers an opportunity to release ourselves from what limits us and thus open our ourselves and our minds to the unknown and uncertainties while embracing transcendence (Braud & Anderson, 1998). I argue that in these moments of 'oneness', we (therapist and client) are entangled in a universal searching and recognition of ourselves and beyond in all our entirety – resulting in a potential releasing of ourselves from boundaries (Rowan & Jacobs, 2002), instead embracing a communion and recognition that we are not merely created but are also the 'manifestation of a greater essence' (Braud & Anderson, 1998, p.112).

This issue of the personal and professional roles of the therapist in relation to client reactions is an important one, which just like the phenomenon that is therapist self-disclosure, does not lead to a definitive answer. Instead, it raises more hermeneutic questions. Braud and Anderson (1998, p.113) state: 'Is there an essence of life and reality or only what we perceive them to be.' In my view, as therapists we need to possess a willingness to embrace 'not knowing', 'uncertainties' and 'uncomfortability' while trusting the process and remaining open to working with the responses, reactions and 'consequences' (Wachtel, 2008). Ultimately, how therapists choose to wrestle with the tensions between their personal and professional roles in relation to client reactions, will always remain a fundamentally subjective experience. In my view, it feels necessary to always be aware of these tensions and position them consciously alongside the notion that 'whenever the mind attempts to understand the essence of the transcendent realm, it always ends in paradox' (Braud & Anderson, 1998, p.113).

Chapter 5
Empirical insights and psychological implications

Research has consistently shown that therapist self-disclosure positively influences clients' perceptions of the therapeutic process. To be more specific, it points to an immediate correlation between therapists' self-disclosure and their clients' view of them as being more relatable and human, thus encouraging them to reciprocate with their own self-disclosures (Knox et al., 1997; Knox & Hill, 2003). This dynamic fosters a therapeutic environment where clients feel understood and accepted, thereby enhancing the therapeutic alliance and normalising clients' experiences and difficulties (Bugental, 1987).

Impact on the Therapeutic Relationship and Client Perception

Myers and Hayes (2006) and Tantillo (2004) assert that clients generally find immediate self-disclosure by therapists more acceptable, probably owing to the focus on the relational dynamics it brings about and clients' assimilation of therapist's reactions to their interpersonal behaviours. This form of self-disclosure can significantly contribute to a deeper relational engagement between therapist and client, although it carries the risk of making the therapist feel vulnerable or judged (Audet, 2011; Farber, 2006). The process of self-disclosure is co-created and fosters empathy, warmth, credibility, and may also open up the space for other positive considerations within the therapeutic relationship (Stolorow et al., 1987; Knox & Hill, 2003).

Empirical Evidence on Client Outcomes

A study by Barrett and Berman (2001) involving Caucasian undergraduate students indicates that therapists who self-disclosed in response to client disclosures were perceived more favourably and were associated with increased client well-being. Nevertheless, a criticism of the study was that it demonstrated a lack of consideration to the content of the disclosures, which it was argued could significantly influence the outcomes. Additionally, the marginalised sample size rendered the findings ungeneralisable. Knox et al. (1997) emphasises the benefits of helpful therapist self-disclosure, noting that it allows clients to see their therapists as human, which helps normalise their own experiences and strengthens the therapeutic relationship. Nevertheless, this study has been criticised for its one-sided approach and neglect of the potential negative impacts resulting from unhelpful therapist self-disclosure.

Long-term Effects and Ethical Considerations

The long-term effects of therapist self-disclosure on client personal growth and the therapeutic relationship are mixed and warrant further research (Audet, 2011; Farber, 2006; Gibson, 2012; Knox et al., 1997; Knox & Hill, 2003). Moreover, ethical considerations, such as maintaining appropriate therapist-client boundaries and the extent of therapists' professional skills, are crucial when evaluating its use. The complexities involved in defining and categorising self-disclosure, including its frequency, types, and outcomes, make it a challenging area to explore empirically (Audet, 2011; Farber, 2006; Gibson, 2012; Knox et al., 1997; Knox & Hill, 2003).

Frequency and Authentic Connection

Therapist self-disclosure used judiciously and infrequently appear to be of beneficence, thus creating an authentic connection whilst fostering an egalitarian relationship (Rogers, 1951; Peterson, 2002), Audet (2011) argues that it is self-disclosures which involve low to moderate levels of intimacy and resonate with clients' experiences and needs that are successful in enhancing the emerging therapeutic relationship. This view is supported by other researchers, highlighting the nuanced and context-dependent nature of effective self-disclosure (Farber, 2006; Gibson, 2012; Knox et al., 1997; Peterson, 2002; Knox & Hill, 2003).

In summary, while therapist self-disclosure can significantly enhance the therapeutic process by fostering deeper connections and normalising client experiences, it must be used judiciously, sparingly and ethically. Further research is needed to fully understand its long-term effects and to refine guidelines for its appropriate use in therapy.

Chapter 6
The Therapist's Use of Self and The Wounded Healer

I find Rowan and Jacobs' (2002) contribution interesting, as it potentially offers a unique understanding of 'self-disclosure' and, by implication, therapist self-disclosure. They identify three therapeutic positions: Instrumental, Relational and Transpersonal. Firstly, the instrumental position, here Rowan and Jacobs (2002) recognise the client's need to be helped and potentially learn tasks and coping strategies aimed at supporting them to manage themselves. This level has a cognitive-behavioural focus and has an emphasis on the client's need for practical support and guidance.

Secondly, they argue that the relational position requires authentic engagement and has strong ties with the person-centred approach (Rowan and Jacobs, 2002). In this position, the client and therapist are more concerned with exploring the client's processes and ways of being and relating at a deeper level.

Finally, the transpersonal level. This involves a relinquishing of boundaries and focuses on the spiritual aspect of relating with self-and-self, self-and-other and beyond. In this sense, the transpersonal level encourages explorations that go beyond the individual's psyche, thus striving towards transcendence. As such, Rowan and Jacobs'

(2002) model points to the therapist's use of self, involving different ways of relating with the client, which also impacts the therapeutic relationship and can extend to differing realms of consciousness, therefore offering a more holistic approach. Their framework provides some guidance on how to hold mindfully albeit 'loosely' to ethics, practice and therapeutic appropriateness when engaging in therapist self-disclosure as well as considering *'what'* and *'why'* therapists choose to disclose.

Although the instrumental position is important within the holistic presentation of the client and therapeutic relationship, I find myself drawn to the relational and, by extension, the transpersonal positions, which advocate that 'personal involvement is much more acceptable, with the therapist much more closely identified with the client and more openly concerned to explore the therapeutic relationship' (Rowan & Jacobs, 2002, p.6). Here, the above-held view is indicative of the two-way process and the possible impact therapist self-disclosure may have on the therapist, client and the therapeutic relationship. Rowan and Jacobs (2002) explore the interactive nature of therapist self-disclosure with a view to how the therapist uses him/herself in the service of healing for the client. Hence, therapist self-disclosure involves the therapist's selective accounts, emotional contributions, countertransference responses, embodied experiences, and verbal and non-verbal ways of relating to their client. Their (Rowan and Jacobs 2002) perspective makes clear the need for therapists to remain rigorous in their constant assessment of *'what'* and *'why'* they choose to disclose, by stating:

> ***'We look at ways in which the therapist is aware of and uses her/his emotions, thoughts and reactions in the service of understanding the client in creating a relationship that serves the client... we look at views on what the therapist might choose to disclose of these reactions or even what the therapist chooses to disclose in the way of personal information' (Rowan & Jacobs, 2002, p.29).***

It can be argued that similarities exist between the third position, the transpersonal and the concept of therapist self-disclosure, in that the former allows for the potential manifestation of therapist and client self-disclosures as 'I-Thou' (Buber, 1958) moments encased in a realm of transcendental mysticism. Moreover, the transpersonal, just like self-disclosure, provides a sense of the 'mystic realm' entangled in an ambience of 'not knowing' and 'mysticism'. For me, both these phenomena appear to echo subtle and not-so-subtle undertones of 'taboo', and what could be deemed unchartered territory for many therapists. I make this integrative link between 'therapist self-disclosure' and the transpersonal, acknowledging their fluid nature because both phenomena are:

> ***'Interested in a way of being, [*in which*] the boundaries between therapist and client may fall away. Both may occupy the same space at the same time, at the level of what is sometimes termed 'soul', sometimes 'heart' and sometimes 'essence': what they have in common is a willingness to let go of all aims and assumptions" (Rowan & Jacobs, 2002, p.59).***

In view of the above, it can be suggested that these 'organic' moments of therapist self-disclosure - although rare - are spontaneous, potentially accidental, unintentional and mystical. To my mind, the above quotation highlights the ambiguities associated with this phenomenon and brings to the fore concerns regarding relational dynamics, power imbalances, as well as opportunities for both therapist and client to work at relational depth (Mearns & Cooper, 2005). Moreover, the therapist's humanity and subjectivity are intrinsically linked with their use of self and their stance on and use of therapist self-disclosure.

As Kaiser (1997, p.74) acknowledges, 'the very nature of clinical work is such that a practitioner's primary tool is him - or her - self'. As a result, the therapist (as does the client) already enters the therapeutic space exempt from neutrality and in full possession of their beliefs, values, educational and training experiences, developmental histories, personality and life experiences (Kaiser,1997). Therefore, in view of this non-neutral stance, it can be argued that the therapist's use of self plays a significant role in relation to its appropriateness and therapeutic application within the 'frame' of therapist self-disclosure and the service of healing for the client.

Owing to the complexity involved in the application of therapist self-disclosure, the various schools of thought urge caution, arguing that therapist self-disclosure be employed when the therapist is clear in its therapeutic benefit for the client (Brown & Walker, 1990; Goldfried et al, 2003; Lane & Hull, 1990; Mahalik et al, 2000; Zahm, 1998). Existing research highlights this ambiguity, as research findings often appear conflictual and contradictory (Audet, 2011; Gibson, 2012; Farber, 2006; Knox et al, 1997; Knox & Hill, 2003).

Therapist as 'Wounded Healer'

Considering psychotherapy's continuous evolution, what becomes apparent is that the notion of the 'mysterious' therapist has been superseded by a subjective, human other, who through conscious awareness is closely in touch with their own shadow (Rowan & Jacobs, 2002). Hence, Baldwin's (2000, p. 36), observation of Roger's (1961) focus on the therapist acknowledging him/herself as 'an imperfect person with flaws which make him/her vulnerable'. This suggests that to dismiss this profound reality may create an avenue in which the therapist's use of self-disclosure may become self-indulgent, grandiose and unethical. Furthermore, it may result in therapy proving anti-therapeutic and harmful to the client's ability to access opportunities for healing. In reference to the imperfect and flawed being/therapist (Miller & Baldwin, 2000), I make an integrative link between the fluid, authentic essence of therapist self-disclosure when viewed in combination with the therapist as a 'wounded healer' (Jung, 1993). The above notion highlights the creative component born out of self-disclosure, which is also present within human interaction. In this respect, holding the shadow and the luminosity, it is helpful to note that within the therapeutic relationship 'it is what therapists do with their woundedness that is important' (McBeath, 2019 cited in Marais and McBeath, 2021, p. 8). Indeed, Miller and Baldwin (2000, p. 258) remark that 'creativity is constantly renewed despite, or perhaps because of, the wounded-healer's vulnerability'.

Consequently, there is a sense of the power encompassed within the therapist's use of self and therapist self-disclosure, in relation to the transformation of wounds in the service of healing. Guntrip (1968) acknowledges the duality incumbent in therapist self-disclosure, declaring that the practice and process of psychotherapy possibly serves as a healing experience for both therapist and client.

The literature review, historical context and empirical research acknowledge the benefits of therapist self-disclosure for the client, notwithstanding its challenges and dangers. Within this frame exists the inescapable notion of therapist self-disclosure allied with the concept of the therapist as the 'wounded healer' (Jung, 1993). Hill (1993) recognises the impact of therapist self-disclosure on the disclosing therapist, stating that these moments are possibly experienced as signs of personal and professional growth, leading to more enjoyable, interesting engagement and explorations of self-with-self and self-with-other. The Jungian perspective draws attention to the collective archetype of the wounded healer (Jung, 1993), which to my mind correlates with therapist self-disclosure. It argues that therapists need to support clients to experience them as ordinary, flawed and fallible human beings so that they can internalise their therapist as a healing presence and, through this integration, meet their own inner healer (Samuels, 1985).

Summary

The literature review has explored various texts, historical and empirical evidence to provide a healthy flavour of the range of complexities and understandings of therapist self-disclosure. The benefits of therapist self-disclosure are presented, as are the disadvantages and challenges it brings. Furthermore, the impact of holding a non-disclosing stance is also considered. To honour the duality incumbent in this phenomenon, the therapist's use of self (Rowan & Jacobs, 2002) and the 'wounded healer' (Jung, 1993) in relation to therapist self-disclosure, has also been put forward. Thus, therapist self-disclosure's contribution can be viewed in this same vein, as it is considered disadvantageous by some and beneficial by others. Subsequently, Peterson (2002) implores us to reflect on ethical considerations when deciding on risks and merits.

However, given the extensive studies carried out in the name of self-disclosure and, more specifically, therapist self-disclosure (Audet & Everall, 2003; Farber, 2006; Gibson, 2012; Hanson, 2005; Knox et al, 1997, Knox & Hill, 2003; Meyers & Hayes, 2006; Peterson, 2002; Tantillo, 2004), one particular aspect remains unchartered: the therapists' personal experience of *their* self-disclosures and the impact it may have on them. This is the central focus of this book.

Chapter 7
Wrestling with the Ambiguity and Complexity of Self-Disclosure

This chapter attempts to arrive at an understanding of what constitutes self-disclosure and acknowledges this subject matter's ambiguous nature and complexities. Consequently, self-disclosure is a very wide umbrella term and is problematic to define. This chapter provides insight into therapist's accounts, citing examples of therapist self-disclosure in many different forms, thereby making explicit its existence at multi-levels within human interpersonal exchange. These examples and experiences of therapist self-disclosure are by no means exhaustive, but do provide valuable insight into therapists' understanding, experience and conceptualisation of this phenomenon.

There appears to be consensus among therapists regarding the ambiguity and complexity of self-disclosure. The phenomenon is understood and experienced in unique ways by all therapists, hence, highlighting this phenomenon's essentially subjective quality. What is clearly evident is the difficulty of holding the term self-disclosure within a definitive frame. This is evident in the following comments:

> **Gabriella said: *'It's a really fine line and I, dunno... sometimes self-disclosure in itself is a concept that can, you know, mean so many different things for different people.***

> ***Something that is, um, meant to be kept behind doors or something, like the disclosing of information, or you know… it… it's usually used in those kind of terms, you know, like a more legal or administrative term.'***

The above comment demonstrates the therapist's own struggle to arrive at a clearly defined understanding of this phenomenon. Gabriella's further comment ***'I think self-disclosure is quite loaded'*** to my mind captures the very essence of this complexity.

Cristina's understanding of self-disclosure shares the same struggle.

> **Cristina said:** ***'It's a whole science and, and an art actually.'***

Furthermore, she emphasises its complexity as she stated it has ***'so many different parameters'.*** Cristina's contribution gives an indication that she is constantly grappling with this subject matter. This sense of struggle is further reinforced when she outlined her process of working with such a complex concept.

> **Cristina said:** ***'So again, what is a disclosure? How do you define it? There's so many different elements of, of it, erm, so again, doing something can be equally, erm, speaks volumes, as not doing anything.'***

Anna's view of what self-disclosure is correlates with the above perceptions.

> **Anna said:** ***'I don't really have a very clear theory around it.'***

Her comment points to the challenge all therapists face when working with this subject matter. Anna went on to acknowledge the complexity of self-disclosure.

> **Anna said:** ***'I've just spoken about emotional disclosure, really, and then there is (pause), for me, perhaps I should have started with the fact that there are different types of disclosure.'***

Jack's contribution to the notion of what self-disclosure also points to the challenge it presents to therapists while highlighting the need to provide a sense of a definition, even if it is a personal one.

> **Jack said:** ***'Well on a very basic level, it's obviously revealing something about yourself or your experiences that you p'rhaps wouldn't tell many people, or that you find, consider to be rather sensitive material, erm. What is my sense of self-disclosure? I think it's something that's quite precious and not to be banded around, not to be played with.'***

Similarly to other views, Jack's process demonstrates his need to be reflective of what this phenomenon actually is. His use of the word ***'basic'*** can be understood to signify that many different formulations of this complex phenomenon exist. He offered a sense that pinning it down in a defined framework remains impossible. Therapists appear contradictory in their perception of self-disclosure. Furthermore, there is suggestion in Jack's statement that he favours a cognitive understanding and exploration of this phenomenon, which is perhaps at odds with the very subjective nature in which self-disclosures often occur. In this respect, Jack's view that self-disclosures should not consist of ***'sensitive material'*** provides evidence of how subjectivity adds potential struggle to these well-thought-out cognitive contributions. This point is illustrated in Jack's very real and authentic human account below.

> **Jack said:** ***'My own certain episodes, in my own life, that have been difficult, challenging, I've sometimes shared. Not often but I've shared, found it useful to share, and I've checked it with my supervisor, useful to share for the***

> ***benefit of the client (pause). Um, one or two very, very sensitive areas or episodes, not in great detail.'***

His emphasis and repetition of the word **'useful'** is symbolic of his professional and ethical awareness that self-disclosure is to be applied primarily for client benefit. Jack's contradiction, in terms of sharing sensitive material while also stating that therapist self-disclosure should not contain sensitive material, is perhaps demonstrative of the struggle to hold the tensions within this phenomenon. His comment suggests a need to establish a cognitive understanding of the workings of this phenomenon, which, owing to the added complexity of human subjectivity, is not always possible. In common with the above viewpoints, Miles' quote suggests that he recognises this complexity.

> **Miles said: *'I think when you disclose, it's a big umbrella term' and 'it's very, erm, risky, tricky water'.***

The above narratives all highlight the uncertainty that exists within self-disclosure. There is an illusiveness about this subject matter that can potentially manifest insecurities within the disclosing therapist. Alongside this is a strong sense that therapists struggle with self-disclosure's definition and what it constitutes. Hence, Gabriella's comment.

> **Gabriella said: *'It's a really fine line and I don't know, sometimes self-disclosure in itself is a concept that can, you know, mean so many different things for different people.'***

I empathise with the above-mentioned therapist viewpoints and understand their struggle to pin down the very personal and unique interpretations of what self-disclosure represents for them, as individuals. These ambiguities potentially give rise to vulnerabilities, which centre around its use, its benefit for the client, its impact on their own sense of professionalism, ethical considerations and their personal self. The subliminal message and fear in their respective narratives - **'Have I done something wrong? Have I revealed too much?**

Can this be used against me personally, professionally, legally?' - are very evident. Their accounts are indicative of the therapist's need to be very reflective and thoughtful about engaging in therapist self-disclosure. The exploration of this subject matter has produced valuable insight regarding complexities in the form of various types of self-disclosure, which in turn have implications for the notion of therapist self-disclosure. Furthermore, it alerts one to the fact that subjectivity is always in the frame – and especially highlights and questions the expectation that therapist self-disclosure is always 'reflected' upon and 'thought-through'.

Chapter 8
Types of self-disclosure

Existing research, literature, empirical studies and therapists accounts all provide evidence that self-disclosure is multi-layered and that this phenomenon exists in many forms. What constitutes self-disclosure is also influenced by the individual's personal understanding, experience and impact in relation to this subject matter. To engage in a thorough exploration of the various types of self-disclosure (which are by no means exhaustive), it will be important to make a distinction between intentional and unintentional self-disclosure.

Intentional Therapist Self-Disclosure

For the purposes of this discussion, intentional therapist self-disclosure can be defined as when the therapist intentionally and sometimes explicitly discloses information that has been thought through, considered and pre-meditated, either in the moment of disclosing or prior to that moment. In this sense, and from therapists' accounts, intentional therapist self-disclosure will include non-immediate, selective and subjective therapist self-disclosures. It is important to note that the above-mentioned types of therapist self-disclosure, incorporated under the umbrella term of 'intentional self-disclosure', can present verbally and non-verbally within the therapist-client relationship.

Cristina's comment is demonstrative of her intentional and yet selective disclosure.

> **Cristina said: *'Women can experience that.'***

In the above response, there is a sense that for Cristina's self-disclosure to be of benefit to her client, it needs to be depersonalised, hence the reference to 'women' and the omission of 'I'.

> **Gabriella said: *'I think it's quite common for people to ask me where I'm from and I don't, um, nowadays, I don't have a problem answering that or, you know, that I grew up in a different country. I don't go into details where my parents are from, where I was born... those kind of things are more complicated.'***

Gabriella's response is interesting because of her awareness of the non-verbal and transparent disclosure already evident – i.e. that she is foreign and different from many clients she may work with, on a cultural and national level. Her comment suggests that in past experiences, self-disclosure at this level may have felt problematic - hence her comment **'nowadays I don't have a problem answering'**. Within her intentional and selective self-disclosure, there is evidence of a subtle and necessary boundary, as she is wary not to go into too much detail. She affirmed this by saying: **'I don't go into details.'** Her acknowledgment of the complexity encompassed in this phenomenon is illustrated in her choice of words, **'more complicated',** which can be understood as her means of keeping therapist self-disclosures to the point and within boundaries. This emphasis on detail is repeated by other therapists.

> **Anna said: *'The disclosure has to be very, very general, nothing terribly personal.'***

Anna's response reinforces an apparent consensus surrounding the need to maintain boundaries in relation to therapist self-disclosure. Her repetition of the word **'very'** indicates her insistence on the need to adhere to boundaries. Furthermore, her response alluded to the level of content shared. Evidence for this comes in her use of the word **'general'** and her rule that disclosures do not involve the therapist's personal aspects. Moreover, her response may also be indicative of the therapist's need to put in place self-protecting boundaries regarding themselves and their personal material. This sentiment is further expounded in Anna's comment below.

> **Anna said:** ***'I disclose very little about my personal life, but if the client asks then I am quite honest but explore why they want to know first.'*** **Anna continued:** ***'If a person says to me, "I wonder what you think about children, and do you have any?" I would ask them first, "Why do you ask?" And, "What would that mean for you if I did or didn't?" But, in general, I don't disclose anything of myself.'***

Anna's response shows something of her process of assessment regarding disclosure. There is a need to explore with the client their reason for wanting to know information about her, and her assessment is hence based on how she can deliver her disclosure, so that it is of benefit to the client while also remaining protective of her personal piece. Her comment **'in general I don't disclose anything myself'** emphasises her need to uphold boundaries, possibly avoid disclosure, and also highlights her awareness of the risks involved in this grey area of exploration. Nevertheless, as with the other participants, Anna's approach to therapist self-disclosure appears contradictory at times, as demonstrated in the following remark illustrating countertransference therapist self-disclosure.

> **Anna said:** ***'I would let my emotions show, somebody who was sharing something very sad, I might really up the empathy and... so disclose that it really felt that sad for me too.'***

Anna's response again illustrates the complexity of this phenomenon, as her struggle between disclosing and non-disclosure mirrors the fluidity encompassed in therapist self-disclosure. There is a suggestion in her words that sharing countertransference self-disclosures is more acceptable. Miles holds a slightly different view in relation to intentional therapist self-disclosure, a standpoint that can be gleaned from his response below.

> **Miles said:** ***'Keep it short and curly, and only share stuff that you are really comfortable with in the public domain. I think that's key because otherwise it will come out wrong. So it's about parts of your story, parts of yourself that you are comfortable with people knowing.'***

Here, Miles' response echoes Gabriella and Anna's view that the therapist needs to uphold boundaries in relation to the level of detail being shared. He acknowledges the need for the therapist to be comfortable with sharing their disclosure and the content involved. His comment also hints at his awareness of the risks presented by self-disclosure, as it could **'come out wrong'**, thus potentially resulting in ruptures to the relationship, the work, as well as emotional injuries for both client and therapist.

Intentional therapist self-disclosure also extends to countertransference self-disclosures, which have been ever so subtly alluded to in Anna's expression of emotional self-disclosure. Miles recognises that different schools of thought hold different views on self-disclosure. Hence, experience, training and theoretical orientation also play a part in therapists' decisions regarding its use.

> **Miles said:** ***'It's about, you have to risk how you experience the client, you have to risk your countertransference because you give them a different take on how they come across, in a way that probably people outside don't risk.'***

> **Miles said:** ***'I know more kind of relational psychoanalytical people would share some stuff, they wouldn't share***

> ***their stuff. They would share their countertransference, that's it. But if I think of the humanistic psychotherapist, I think sometimes you have to risk something of yourself.'***

Miles' response is illustrative of the benefits of countertransference therapist self-disclosure for the client. He uses the word **'risk'** repeatedly and thus conveys an impression that disclosure in any form involves risk and needs to be cautiously applied, with the therapist always conscious of this risk. Miles opines that sometimes therapists need to find the courage to enter that 'intimate edge of exchange' (Ehrenberg, 1995) for their disclosures to be of service to their client. There is a sense that clients need to feel met by their therapist and this requires the therapist to give something of themselves, something of a more personal and private nature, for the clients to trust, connect, engage in the work and enter into moments of working at relational depth (Mearns & Cooper, 2005). Miles' narrative draws attention to the different types of therapist self-disclosure when he said: ***'I think sometimes we have to explicitly disclose or we subtly disclose'.*** His words **'subtly disclose'** offers evidence of the various levels relating to self-disclosure.

Unintentional Therapist Self-Disclosure

For the purposes of this study, unintentional therapist self-disclosure will include implicit self-disclosures, embodied self-disclosures, as well as accidental and unavoidable self-disclosures. These variations give texture to the notion that self-disclosure is constant. This is not to suggest that its constancy lies in this domain only - it is simply that unintentional self-disclosure adds a more tangible flavour to the notion of the constancy involved in therapist self-disclosure. Therapists seem to acknowledge the constancy pertaining to self-disclosure and highlight that disclosures can be unintentional, environmental and that sometimes they occur in moments that are simply out of our hands. In reference to Freud's (1912) contribution to the subject – that a therapist should be a mirror and reflect back what the client projects

– Miles' response offers a more complex appreciation of the multi-faceted processes involved in self-disclosure.

> **Miles said:** ***'I think what he (Freud) overlooks is that we are constantly giving out information, implicitly through our tone of voice, vitality of emotion and how it is expressed, our body language, even the position behind the couch, you pick up an awful lot from people's energetic field.'***

Cristina shares Miles' view, as illustrated in her comment below.

> **Cristina said:** ***'There's a lot of body expression that I have learned over the years to contain… The people I work with are British, they're much more contained, so I don't, I, you know, it doesn't feel very natural to be very animated with them, and sometimes if I am animated with them, that is self-disclosure.'***

Cristina's contribution acknowledges the implicit embodied expression that can be aroused in moments of therapist self-disclosure. She went on to state that ***'self-disclosure is constant'*** and elaborated on this in her comment below.

> **Cristina said:** ***'It can be absolutely anything that you carry in you… All the time, absolutely all the time and we take it for granted.'***

Her repetitive use of words such as **'absolutely'** and phrases such as **'all the time'** demonstrates that she sees that self-disclosure is always in the frame, which correlates with the view that we are always giving away something of ourselves in the intersubjective exchange (Stolorow et al, 1987). Her point is that, even without verbally and intentionally communicating a disclosure, we are always self-disclosing in the sharing/exchange. Cristina continues to point out this constancy:

Cristina said: ***'A sharing again comes from what I wear, how I sit, how I move my hands, you know. My culture shows, my accent shows, everything about me shows, that I'm not, you know… that difference is there and I'm identifiable, um, I'm disclosing something about who I am.'***

The above perspective is also shared by Gabriella, as is evident in her remarks below.

Gabriella said: ***'My accent, you know, people wonder a lot, "Where do you come from? What language do you speak? Why are you here, um, in London?"'***

She went on to acknowledge that ***'it was obvious that I also came from a different country'.***

Gabriella's contribution lends further weight to the idea of self-disclosure's constancy and highlights the impossibility of neutrality existing within this frame. There is a sense that we are always communicating something implicitly, in our way of being with the other and this does not always need to involve words. Cristina reverberates the above view, as there is a sense that implicit therapist self-disclosure is an inevitable and unavoidable part of the human exchange. Miles and Anna's perspectives complement the above view regarding self-disclosure's constancy and the impossibility of neutrality existing in these moments.

Cristina said: ***'I think my self-disclosure would be more with a nodding or be more with a smile'.***

She went on to say: ***'When I do it as an implicit kind of way of a nodding or a smile, then it's genuine, because I wouldn't just do it in any other way, it needs to be genuine and there's that implicit communication, that how, how can we look at it in a more healthy way.'***

> **Anna said*: 'You always disclose something of yourself, you always do and if somebody comes to your house there is disclosure... there's always gonna be something that shows, erm, that you're a human being and that you are not a machine, so there's always something, some disclosure, um, and I think it is about the balance of, um, having rules and boundaries, safety... Some disclosure is inevitable, there'll always be the mask that slips down.'***

Anna's perspective elaborates on this unquestionable constancy as she understands it to stem from our essentially subjective, human nature. Hence, her need to acknowledge the importance of balance, boundaries, rules and safety, which in her view, is experienced, to a degree, as a lesser danger when the individual is faced with a machine. For me, there is a naive notion of **'safety'** in relation to machinery that comes through in her statement. In this age of social media, it can be argued that danger exists even more so, and then again, these dangers exist largely because they are 'powered' by human beings. To my mind, self-disclosure and human interaction can also present as an enmeshment with machines (e.g. computers, Skype, Zoom, etc) – and even within this frame, self-disclosure remains inevitable and risky.

Anna acknowledges the implicit constancy of therapist self-disclosure, as is evident in her remark below.

> **Anna said: *'We never spoke French but, on occasion, she would use French expressions. We had a bit of a knowing look together, um, (laugh), so it was perhaps a corrective experience when I could say I could understand you even if you speak in a different language.'***

Anna's example of implicit self-disclosure is indicative of the fact that disclosure is always in the room. There is a sense that we are always giving out something of ourselves, even when this is not the intention. What is clear is that, within these very human moments, there appears to be a somewhat involuntary, automatic, spontaneous exchange - further evidence of the constancy and fluidity embroiled in this phenomenon. These aspects - 'spontaneous', 'accidental' and 'involuntary' therapist self-disclosures - are further illustrated in Miles' experience of implicit self-disclosure. Miles' response below is evidence of the subtle, sensitive and empathic interplay that 'embodies' this phenomenon. His experience lends support to the notion of constancy encompassed in self-disclosure.

> **Miles said:** ***'Sometimes the client just knows things about us implicitly that doesn't need to be explicated.'***

Here, Miles' contribution resonates strongly with Anna's sense of the **'implicit knowing'** involved. This notion of 'implicit knowing' is very apparent in Miles' comment below.

> **Miles said:** ***'I wonder, at an implicit level, they know something about us already, so you know, could that be a kind of an amber light asking for something, something they feel but they don't know explicitly about us?'***

> **Miles goes on to say:** ***'But also those subtle moments when the client is picking something up implicitly and you can feel they're almost saying, mm, mm, am I picking this up right? You have to take the risk, I think.'***

There is a sense here that sometimes implicit self-disclosures guide both therapist and client in the journey, but also holds therapists accountable to the boundaries involved when implicitly (or explicitly) disclosing. Miles also conveys an awareness of the sense of risk that is ever-present in therapist self-disclosure. His repetitive use of non-verbal embodied expressions **'mm', 'mm'** are demonstrations of the non-verbal signals that are automatic and organic in a symbolic sense of communion with the other. Within this context of unintentional and implicit therapist self-disclosure, moments occur when these disclosures manifest as accidental, spontaneous and unavoidable. These forms of therapist self-disclosure have been corroborated by therapists who engage with self-disclosure wittingly and unwittingly and further underscore the notion of constancy in relational to self-disclosure.

> **Miles said:** ***'But sometimes, I think, those moments, a more intuitive sense is at play or there is something transferentially at play that makes you say something.'***

It can be argued that Miles' response is suggestive of the transpersonal and transcendental elements that manifest and may lead to potential 'I-Thou moments' (Buber,1958).

Miles' comment instructs us to bear in mind that an infinite array of factors is present in the therapeutic space in which self-disclosure is just but one element. Hence, there is the powerful resonance of the client's transferential projections, emotional traumas and wounds that sometimes require an intuitive and spontaneous response from the therapist. To my mind, in these moments, there is the possibility that the therapist's own wounds are called upon in the service of healing. In view of self-disclosures' implicit exchange Miles' view is also shared by other therapists.

> **Cristina said:** ***'I think the nods and smiles come quite automatic. I think it's a natural kind of instinctual reaction, erm, which is driven by the body, it's all kind of, erm, acknowledgement in that moment.'***

Cristina is describing the innate processing involved in these moments of self-disclosure. Her use of words such as **'automatic', 'natural', 'instinctual'** and the phrase **'driven by the body'** all point to the essentially subjective and human interplay, which has a fluid feel, an urgency of meeting in the moment.

> **Cristina added:** ***'Certain things that might come in a little bit natural or automatic, but actually, there's a whole different aspect, um, you know, on its own you take something there that is just a bit, but then that bit is massive.'***

Her use of the word 'massive' adds weight to her perception of the power and risk that hover over these intimate moments.

Miles' outlook supports Cristina's perception regarding the power and risk that emerges in implicit self-disclosure.

> **Miles said: '*I think sometimes we self-disclose with a sense of immediacy and spontaneity, which can be incredibly powerful, er, in a very moving and intimate way. And other times, it might backfire.*'**

In my view, all accounts conjure up a sense of the gut reaction, the embodied experience, that surfaces in these moments and that in itself is imbued with risk.

Jack offered an interesting revelation here.

> **Jack said: '*So perhaps there is something about spontaneous self-disclosure that I've never thought about.*'**

Here, Jack offers a sense that disclosures can be so natural, instinctive and spontaneous that therapists may not even recognise when they are in the midst of self-disclosing. This notion lends support to the view that therapists appear to need to potentially understand self-disclosure as a clinical term and in this sense it involves a focus on cognition – hence the expectation of always needing to be carefully considered. Reducing self-disclosure to this rather narrow view negates its complexity and the human, subjective involvement that take place in these moments. This underlying need to hold to a procedure, criteria and framework in itself can be considered to be the therapist's means of attempting to manage this fluid and changeable phenomenon as a way to reducing risk and increasing safety for both parties. Therapists also acknowledge that experiences in which their self-disclosures came in the form of unavoidable, accidental, spontaneous and involuntary communicative displays were inevitable given our essentially human and subjective nature.

> **Gabriella said:** ***'Sometimes, unavoidably, you will be throwing things out at them or you know, things that you're not feeling that well or you're ill or coughing or you, I don't know, sniff... When that happens, it has a level of spontaneity or of, you know, feeling kind of, er, risk-taking.'***

Furthermore, owing to the spontaneous nature of this subject matter, when recalling an experience within the therapist-client dyad, **Gabriella said***:*

> ***'It was kinda like, aaaah, caught by surprise'.***

Gabriella's comments highlight the need for therapists to develop an emotional robustness that would support them to manage and recover from these risky and uncertain moments, so that they are able to remain focused on the client's material and offer the support needed to maintain safety for both.

In light of the above experiences shared by Gabriella, Anna's experience of accidental self-disclosure is indicative of these moments occurring outside of the therapist's control. As Miles has previously indicated, in these moments, there is potentially something somewhat intuitive, transferential and potentially transcendental that may be emerging within the self-disclosure frame.

> **Anna said:** ***'Just very recently I didn't mean to disclose... It wasn't deliberate disclosure, something happened.'***

Anna is referring to a situation in which her client had connected with her on a video call for a therapy session but on the wrong day and at the wrong time. As a result, he saw Anna in a completely different environment than the one she occupies as his therapist. She experienced this accidental self-disclosure as emotionally injurious to herself and, by her own admission, she stated it had changed the dynamic. Her sense was that the transference was broken, and the client was left thinking 'I don't know you'. Her experience highlights the potential pitfalls presented in self-disclosure moments, which are sometimes outside of the therapist's control. Anna goes on to talk about another of her experiences of accidental and spontaneous self-disclosure.

> **Anna said: *'I have another client who, who said, oh her parents lived in um, Avignon, so that's in France, so I asked where because I've lived in France on many occasions. I go to France a lot and she said that they were in Avignon. It slipped out, "Oh how interesting, I know Avignon, my nephew was there" and I thought, "Why did you tell her that? Why did you, um, tell her that."'***

There is a sense of nervousness, worry and curiosity about Anna's summary of this accidental and spontaneous disclosure. As with all therapists 'caught' in these anxiety-provoking moments, a subtly punitive battle appears to be present as they intrapsychically wrestle with their disclosures. They're often left asking themselves*: 'Was that okay?', 'Did I do something wrong?', 'Will this create a rupture?', 'What is my part in this?' and 'Is there something I need to be attending to in my own process?'.* Below, Jack's narrative corroborates this point and he also shares some interesting and unique discoveries.

> **Jack said: *'The implicit as opposed to explicit, erm, perhaps the sense of the therapist you are, giving something without saying it, with a gesture or an expression, so perhaps we're saying it needn't actually be verbal, but it can just be something you co-create, which is felt.'***

Jack's testimony, as do the other therapists', reinforces the notion that implicit self-disclosures, involving gestures and non-verbal components, are constantly being made. He is also mindful of the interpersonal two-way process, as illustrated through his use of the expression **'co-create'.** This is suggestive of an interactive intersubjective meeting, in which both parties engage in dyadic communion. Jack takes this concept a step further by introducing a sense that self-disclosures of this nature resonate with the client's need to 'feel felt' (Stern, 1998).

Jack continues to emphasise the notion of implicit self-disclosure as a therapeutic tool that supports the client's need to feel met. He remarks on the constancy of self-disclosure always being in the frame by saying: ***'We know from the signals that the other person gets it.'*** This implicit, embodied sense of self-disclosure is further expressed in his next quote, which refers to situations where he risked offering comforting touches/gestures to his clients.

> **Jack said***: **'I didn't say anything, I just done that*** (referring to placing his hand on a client's shoulder)***, so maybe there, perhaps with certain work, certain contexts, certain clients, it's more constant than with others.'***

His repeated use of the word **'certain'** gives the impression that - as with each client, context and relational ways of being - each disclosure also holds a uniqueness that cannot be replicated or revisited in the same way. For me, even given the infinite types of self-disclosure and the risks involved, I note that there exists an underlying sense of embracing the magic of the moment that therapists subtly, implicitly and explicitly allude to at times. Discussions on this subject highlight the element of risk, which exists at many levels and which will be explored in the following chapter.

This chapter focused on how therapists understood, viewed, thought about and interpreted what 'self-disclosure' meant for them. Therapists' accounts evidence the complexity involved in this phenomenon. Consequently, what constitutes self-disclosure is variable and personal to the therapist's unique experience and interpretation. It is interesting to note that most therapists hold an awareness of self-disclosure and yet simultaneously find themselves wrestling with the concept at different levels when dialoguing about this subject matter. Therapists' accounts discussed in this book are representative of an awareness that self-disclosure involves risk, vulnerability and sometimes comes at a cost to the disclosing therapist (personally, professionally, ethically).

Furthermore, Cristina describes self-disclosure as being constant and states that it happens ***'all the time, absolutely all the time and***

we take it for granted'. This view is shared by many therapists. Most therapists agree that therapist self-disclosure appears to benefit the client and therapeutic relationship. Moreover, moments of therapist self-revelation appear to invite relational depth and intimacy between therapist and client. Nevertheless, it can be argued that the opposite is also possible depending on the client's perception, interpretation, readiness and receptivity for such encounters. These views link well with empirical studies (Audett & Everall, 2003); Barrett & Berman, 2001; Knox et al's, 1997; Knox & Hill, 2003; Watkins, 1990) in which explorations into this phenomenon appear to provide evidence of a correlation between therapist self-disclosure and increased therapist likability and connection when applied cautiously and in moderation.

Owing to the complexities involved in self-disclosure, it is clear from the various accounts, literature and empirical studies that numerous types of self-disclosure exist. This variation and complexity pertaining to this phenomenon is also evident in therapists' accounts. The complexity of self-disclosure sub-types is alluded to by Audet and Everall (2003), Gibson (2012), Knox et al (1997) and Farber (2006). In this respect, there is consensus within therapists' accounts, the existing knowledge base encapsulated in the literature review and empirical evidence that self-disclosure is problematic to define. How therapist self-disclosure is understood is personal to the individual therapist, as it involves a complex interplay of ***'everything they carry in them'***. Indeed, Kaiser (1997) states that the therapist's history, experience, personality, education and culture is always in the frame.

Regarding intentional and unintentional self-disclosure, therapists seem to acknowledge that therapist self-disclosure occurs in moments where psychological space is available to allow for assessment, thinking through and following a personal 'criterion', as well as existing in moments where the instinctual, automatic and spontaneous nature of therapist self-disclosure manifested. It is important to note that therapist self-disclosure is not always premeditated or privy to assessment. As noted in this chapter, one therapist surprised himself by discovering that self-disclosure can occur spontaneously. Discussions on this phenomenon acknowledge that when therapists talk about self-disclosure, their perception of this concept reflects multi-levelled thinking and an awareness of risk, which is always present. Furthermore, therapists' viewpoints appear to mirror previous research findings that self-disclosure involves intentional and unintentional elements. Moreover, investing this concept illustrates the broadness of this subject matter, which also creates dilemmas for therapists using self-disclosure and wrestling with its complexity.

Therapists appear to be aware of this complexity and the unique 'definitions' ascribed by individual therapists. Although therapist self-disclosure remains constant, more emphasis appears to be placed on its cognitive, thought-through nature, perhaps because this gives therapists an element of control over these very risky moments. It can be argued that owing to the nature of automatic, instinctual and spontaneous self-disclosures, it is very possible for this latter cluster (unintentional therapist self-disclosure) to potentially go unnoticed, hence the impression that, at times, therapists may not even be aware that they are disclosing. Moreover, owing to their specific interpretations, one therapist may consider a moment to be self-disclosure while another therapist may not. These essentially subjective experiences merely amplify the sense of complexity and difficulties involved in wrestling with 'what is self-disclosure'. These various types of self-disclosure all point to the struggle facing therapists when it comes to how they think about, understand, and consciously and unconsciously engage in therapist self-disclosure.

Explorations into the types of therapist self-disclosure led to a consensus among therapists that self-disclosure is a multi-faceted and multi-textured phenomenon. This highlighted the inevitability of, and the insecurity presented by, not always being consciously aware of moments of self-disclosure. While wrestling with this question, similarly to Knox and Hill (2003), therapists recognise that moments of therapist self-disclosure involve other factors, such as guidance, support and empathic challenging. These factors involve the contextual frame and the intrapsychic and interpersonal processes, which are simultaneously in operation during these moments.

Chapter 9
Risks involved in therapist self-disclosure

Therapists acknowledge that therapist self-disclosure is risky and should therefore be applied with caution. The risks involved include those to the therapeutic relationship, the client as well as professional and ethical risks to the therapist.

Decisions for Therapist Self-Disclosure

Decisions for Therapist Self-Disclosure captures all therapists' experience, in terms of the multi-layered processes they engage in when wrestling with the decision to disclose or not to disclose. The uncovered data also indicates that the therapist's training and theoretical orientation impacts their understanding, views and decisions about engaging in therapist self-disclosure. Assessment decisions about therapist self-disclosure involve the therapist having a secure sense of who is sitting in front of them. The client's psychological, emotional and physical presentation is an important factor. These assessments are ongoing and involve the therapist's decisions regarding the client's availability and readiness to work with self-disclosure. An important consideration lies in the question: *Is the client able to work with self-disclosure and recognise that the therapist is another human being in the room?*

> **Cristina said:** ***'So factors, yeah, factors, factors of readiness, erm, readiness, erm, strength, is the person strong enough to see me as a human being? That I also share a vulnerability and not lose face, um, in the therapy relationship? Um, are they able to hold me as an object in their mind?'***

From Cristina's remark, outlining the criteria behind her decisions on whether to engage in therapist self-disclosure is necessary. A lot of importance is placed on assessing whether or not a client is ready to engage in two-person psychology. This is further emphasised by Cristina's repetitive use of words such as **'factors'**, **'readiness'**, **'strength'** and **'strong'**. These repetitions lead me to wonder whether Cristina's grappling with this subject matter is possibly alluding to her own attempts to convince herself and the other that a discerning structure for engaging in therapist self-disclosure exists and is available. In my view, her attempt to 'create' a 'definitive framework' is evidence of the therapist's need to feel secure within the professional and ethical boundaries of the therapeutic relationship and code of conduct, while simultaneously demonstrating, via their efforts to do so, the complexities involved in the debate surrounding therapist self-disclosure.

Another point worth considering is Cristina's use of the words **'strength'** and **'strong'**, as these words have a subjective feel and highlight the reality that therapist self-disclosure is not clinically defined, but is instead encompassed within an essentially subjective experience. To my mind, this subjective quality would be a point of interest within individual therapist's criteria. Furthermore, Cristina makes a valid point, that if the client is not able to see the therapist as another human being/object in the therapeutic meeting/relationship (and this is often the case when working with individuals who have a strong trauma-based history or personality disorders), then therapist self-disclosure will not be beneficial to engendering client wellbeing and healing.

Moreover, Cristina asserts that by disclosing, the therapist places him/herself in a position of vulnerability. By sharing their self-disclosure, the therapist opens themself up to opportunities, which may leave them feeling judged. This vulnerability may also trigger their unresolved developmental wounds. Although the therapy space is a 'safe' place, Cristina's comment is also a reminder that therapists and clients are essentially all human and, in that sense, fallible. Hence, judgment is always in the frame. Subsequently, her comment concludes with her reiterating that therapist self-disclosure can only be of value when the client is able to use the therapist as a healthy/good selfobject (Kohut,1971). Here, the ethical consideration of whether therapist self-disclosure is of benefit to the client is evident. Simultaneously, there appears to be a hint of the phenomenon's potential risk and impact on the disclosing therapist, which is expressed in the acknowledgement of the therapist's vulnerability. Her comment looks at the client's presentation in relation to the therapist's decisions to engage in therapist self-disclosure. It also highlights another point: how might the client respond to the therapist's self-disclosure? This implies recognition of the potential risks to the therapeutic relationship, the work and the self of therapist - hence the mention of the therapist's vulnerability.

The next quote considers the client's response to therapist self-disclosure.

> **Anna said:** ***'You might be sending out a message of, "Here you are, look at me, I've had your experiences but I'm all sorted out, I'm a therapist but you're not." The client may be quite narcissistic and not want to know anything about you. They may feel that they may receive a message of, "I've no right to be a victim."'***

From Anna's response, I notice that much of the focus of her decision-making on whether to engage in therapist self-disclosure is based on the client's presentation and the client's potential response to the therapist's self-disclosure. There is a sense that Anna is aware of therapist self-disclosure's potential to create ruptures to the therapeutic relationship and the work. Anna's use of the word **'narcissistic'**, in reference to the client's presentation, may also be a subtle attempt to acknowledge the power dynamics that interlink with this phenomenon. Furthermore, her response draws attention to the idea that decisions to engage in therapist self-disclosure are not simple but involve the therapist accessing their assessment skills at various levels within their multifaceted process. When Anna states: ***'You might be sending out a message'*** it begs the question: What is the message on the different levels of relational exchange?

From Anna's contribution, one can ascertain that there is a sense that although several types of self-disclosure exist, when one explicitly, verbally discloses, even these disclosures may have implicit, non-verbal, embodied, ambiguous and subliminal messages. Anna's contribution potentially highlights the ethical and professional risks to the therapist and the work, or more pertinently that some therapists - who are not aware of their shadow or have not resolved their narcissistic developmental injuries - may indulge the notion of being placed on a pedestal. My sense is that Anna is quite wary of self-disclosure and its power and therefore consciously monitors her usage of it, as her need to be there for her client and their needs is of paramount importance to her. Holding this in mind may be perceived as a supportive mechanism in keeping the therapist's process and needs in check, to avoid usurping the client's space and experience. Decisions to engage in therapist self-disclosure alert therapists to risks. Self-disclosure's potential to exacerbate the client's (and therapist's) narcissistic injuries is a real possibility and may prove detrimental to client wellbeing, therapeutic work and the relationship. As a consequence, it may potentially result in enactments, ruptures, disruptions and termination of therapy.

A further point worth considering in relation to client presentation is that therapist self-disclosure can be experienced as therapeutically beneficial in that it can 'normalise' certain experiences (for example: a shared experience of bereavement). Nevertheless, it needs to be weighed carefully and applied cautiously, so as not to minimise the client's experience or problem. As a result, sometimes, in relation to client readiness, it is best to withhold therapist self-disclosures and focus on acknowledging, witnessing and validating the client's experience (Miller, 1995). In this way, the client feels seen and heard and is able to integrate their experience. This last point is further emphasised in Miles' contribution below.

> **Miles said:** ***'I think with certain clients I certainly wouldn't, so for instance, um, people who have lots of um, neglect in childhood or trauma, it's not appropriate.'***

Miles' experience suggests that client presentation is a significant factor in therapist's decisions to engage in therapist self-disclosure. Furthermore, therapists' contributions underline the fact that decisions to engage in therapist self-disclosure are heavily influenced by their training, theoretical orientation, experience and skill.

> **Anna said:** ***'I think there's a part of me that always thinks, there's a part of me when talking to a client, I'm talking to my client, my therapy, my profession, the UKCP, erm, my insurance company, there's a part of me that will always think, um, there's an accountability out there, so it's gonna be pretty bland stuff anyway.'***

Anna uses the word **'profession'**, which suggests that her sense and usage of therapist self-disclosure has links with her training and theoretical orientation. By highlighting **'accountability'** she underscores the risks involved to the therapist when engaging in therapist self-disclosure. Subsequently, although Anna has experienced positive moments of therapist self-disclosure, which have resulted in deepening the connection between herself and her clients, there always remains a part of her that is mindful of the implications for the therapist. I view this point as alluding to the imbalance of confidentiality terms within the therapeutic relationship, in that it is afforded the client and not the therapist. Moreover, Anna's summary of her experience in relation to 'accountability', is perhaps indicative of the therapist's need to and means of 'protecting their stuff' and themselves. This notion of training, skill and experience is further elaborated on by Cristina below.

> **Cristina said:** ***'The value of learning when to stop, of assessing the right time, assessing the right words, assessing being more aware of your emotions, how you phrase your emotions, and, and where to stop, so having the boundaries of experience, that, that experience that is disclosed, but that it is also held, contained, appropriate, necessary, honest, genuine, yet able to not get out of hand.'***

For Cristina, therapist self-disclosure is also connected with practice, experience and therapist skill as well as holding an awareness of the therapist's sense of self. Her emphasis on ***'having the boundaries of experience'*** is an important point, as it brings to the fore the notion that therapist self-disclosure will always involve risks. Thus, as therapists grow in experience, practice, confidence and self-awareness, they are more able to manage these risks. This is an important point in that it signifies the dangers therapist self-disclosure can present for therapists - and more specifically the trainee and newly qualified therapist - who are still in the process of learning their craft. This point is further illustrated in Miles' response below.

> **Miles said:** ***'Cos the training was very clear, no self-disclosure, particularly as a trainee... When I was a trainee, it was always drummed into me, which was very powerful, if you do self-disclosure, three quick things you check, who is it for, keep it short and brief.'***

Miles' quote emphasises the potential ambiguous message trainees receive when 'learning' about this phenomenon. From his response, Miles' understanding of his training on this issue appears to be that one should avoid therapist self-disclosure as a trainee and if one does disclose, ensure you are clear about your reason – that it is for the therapeutic benefit of the client. The contradictory nature of this notion (to disclose or not to disclose) is indicative of the complexities involved in therapist self-disclosure. It also appears misleading, as it implies that a 'checklist' exists, which can be accessed when wrestling with decisions around disclosure and non-disclosure. It can be argued that the term 'therapist self-disclosure' in itself is full of contradictions and complexities and it is interesting that training appears to mirror this incongruity. Miles' contribution highlights the potential ethical dilemma therapists' face and how the risks involved are heightened in the hands of a trainee therapist.

> **Miles said:** ***'I was really taught not to self-disclose, don't share until you've learned the craft of being with someone.'***
>
> **Jack said:** ***'Well, we're trained, aren't we, to use it sparingly if we are going to use it at all.'***

The above comments also indicate that therapist self-disclosure is best utilised within the experienced and skilled therapist's repertoire of therapeutic engagement with clients. This idea adds further texture to the complexities involved in the decision-making process. Miles and Jack's comments lead me to pose this question: *If trainees are taught not to disclose while in training, how does this impact them in the later stages, as qualified therapists, when they find themselves wrestling with and making decisions about self-disclosure with their clients?* Training, experience and client presentation are all significant factors in the therapist's decision-making process. Added to the complexity of this phenomenon and decisions about therapist self-disclosure is the question of *'timing'*. Therapists need to be sensitive about *when* (Spinelli, 2002) it is appropriate and inappropriate to self-disclose, as this factor also involves risk. Below, Anna's remarks are indicative of the importance of consciously holding an awareness of timing when deciding about therapist self-disclosure.

> **Anna said:** ***'The distance between how much I disclose in a relational way, erm, is client appropriate and erm, moment appropriate.'***
>
> **Anna said:** ***'I would definitely not if a client was angry with me, um, it really has to be at that point when, um, the client is in a receptive state and the, er, communication is, um, safe.'***

It is evident from Anna's statements that assessing a client's presentation is imperative and alludes to the safety and vulnerability experienced by both therapist and client in the therapeutic space. Furthermore, making a conscious decision not to engage in therapist self-disclosure, as the timing would prove counter-therapeutic for the client's wellbeing aligns with Spinelli's (2002) notion regarding the importance of *when* to disclose. Decisions are also based on managing and monitoring the risk to the client, therapeutic relationship (rupture) and possibly the therapist's personal and professional self. Anna's responses illustrate her experience and skill around assessing the multifaceted layers involved in therapist self-disclosure. To my mind, Anna's points add weight to the argument that trainees should be deterred from venturing into the area of self-disclosure. This argument follows that trainees wrestling with this subject matter may be completely out of their depth and, therefore, more prone to manifesting risks. The importance of timing, waiting for the appropriate moment to engage in therapist self-disclosure, is underscored by all therapists and suggests that timing in itself can render a disclosure helpful or unhelpful to the client, therapeutic relationship and potentially the therapist. Miles' comment below is, again, demonstrative of 'timing' considerations in therapist self-disclosure.

> **Miles said:** ***'So as I was saying, in the early stages, really creating safety, not self-disclosing personal pieces, but that comes much later in the piece and the journey.'***

The issue of timing is further reiterated by Cristina who stated: ***'I wouldn't disclose very early in therapy'***. Anna also draws emphasis to questions of timing by saying, ***'It's really got to be the right person and the right time.'*** There responses stress the importance of client presentation and timing, and hints at their experience of applying caution and discernment when it comes to self-disclosure, which fall within the multi-layered factors operating simultaneously during the therapist's decision-making process.

Chapter 10
Professional Risks

From the outset it is important to mention that in relation to therapist self-disclosure risks include, but are not limited to, those to safety, the client, to the therapeutic relationship and professional personal risks to the therapists.

> **Miles said: *'Cos risk means vulnerability and something I've appreciated as well, interestingly, the, the greater the intimacy of the relational meeting between therapist and client, the greater the risk. Cos what's at the heart of the risk is the relationship.'***

Miles' comment is revealing of the vulnerability of the therapist, both personally and professionally. Their choice to self-disclose involves them sharing parts of themselves with their clients and relinquishing the power and control they have over some of their material. Although Miles is referring to the power self-disclosure may have over the therapeutic relationship in terms of risk, he also uses the words **'vulnerability'** and **'intimacy'**. These words are associated with risk and may unwittingly be expressions of fear of 'not knowing' what the client will do with the therapist's self-disclosure. The following comments highlight this possibility.

> **Miles stated:** ***'The client has the full right to expect confidentiality from us, but we do not have the right to say to a client I'm sharing something personal about me, but I don't want you share this with anyone else. I think that's wrong, for me ethically, professionally you're burdening the client.'***

> **Jack said:** ***'I don't think you can disclose something and say, but please don't ever tell anybody else I said that, um, and again, it's about the trust between us, you know, don't you? That you're talking about a loved one's suicide, you know, you would only share that with someone who you know would not band it around like a piece of gossip.'***

Both comments remind us that the therapeutic relationship is not symmetrical, and that therapist's self-disclosures are not protected by confidentiality. Hence, relationship differences are an indicator of risks involved in therapist self-disclosure. Therapists affirm that it is sometimes necessary to take these risks, as they may be therapeutically beneficial for the client. Therapists' responses indicate that the level of trust and the strength of the bond within the therapeutic relationship is also a key factor when therapist self-disclosure is in the frame. Jack's remark adds further texture to the notion of risk involved.

> **Jack said:** ***'So it's, it's carefully selected, but the person is also carefully chosen and that's my safety, that's my safety net, really. I know that person well enough to assume that the disclosure wouldn't be abused, and I know that if it were spoken about outside, it wouldn't be damaging to my reputation as a therapist.'***

Jack makes clear that he is wary of the risks involved. His remark also indicates his awareness that the therapeutic relationship is not set on equal footing. His remark, as with others before, illustrates the multifaceted, simultaneous processing and assessment the therapist undertakes when deliberating on the use of therapist self-disclosure within the therapist-client relationship. In addition, Jack's response also outlines the risks regarding client presentation, as he states, ***'the person is also carefully chosen'***. Jack's repetitive use of the word **'carefully'** strongly underscores the element of risk, especially professional risk. His repetition of the word **'safety'** may be an indication of the therapist's vulnerability and a need to be somewhat 'protective' of the information they put out. Jack's acknowledgment that ***'if it were spoken about it wouldn't be damaging to my reputation as a therapist'*** is recognition of the professional risks pertaining to the disclosing therapist.

As with other therapist accounts, Jack's need to ***'know that person well enough'*** is suggestive of the concept of 'timing' involved in therapist self-disclosure. In other words, disclosures are more available to being shared when the therapeutic relationship has been developed over time, as this gives therapists a more secure sense of who is sitting in front of them, and it involves the establishment of 'trust' so ***'that the disclosure will not be abused'*** (**Jack**). Although creating safety is key for the client's process, Jack's response also points to the therapist's need to feel safe in moments of self-disclosure. This again highlights potential professional risks and vulnerabilities associated with this phenomenon. Nevertheless, therapist self-disclosure exists under a complex umbrella. Thus, no matter how much therapists attempt to inoculate themselves from its impact, owing to our essentially human and subjective nature there will always be risks in relation to self-disclosure. Below, Anna's comment sums up the perception of professional risk and highlights the relationship differences, as well as the potential blurring of boundaries tied up in this subject matter.

> **Anna said*****: 'I think there's a lot of risk in there and for the therapy, for the therapy. Is there a lot of risk in the relationship? I think it takes a therapeutic relationship into a personal relationship and that's what worries me, that it's not a personal relationshipness, erm, that's a shame but the person's not paying for a friend.'***

Anna is alerting the reader to hold an awareness of therapist self-disclosure's power to change relationship dynamics, from that of a therapeutic and professional relational frame to one involving the blurring of boundaries, a friendship and potential role reversal. Anna's repetitive use of the word **'risk'** coupled with the word **'worry'** can appear to be suggestive of an expression of fear and anxiety regarding professional conduct, ethical issues and the therapist's self-esteem. This underlying expression of caution is not exempt from any moment in which therapists exercise self-disclosure. Nevertheless, it does highlight the dangers involved in dabbling in this area, especially for a trainee learning the craft and simultaneously wrestling with this phenomenon. Below, Jack's remark reinforces the benefits of limiting therapist self-disclosure as well as acknowledging the asymmetrical relationship.

> **Jack said*: 'I think there can't be total equality between the two because you're coming here, you're paying me, it's my room, it's my business and although I do believe that, I'd be thinking about the client as the expert actually, it's not, we not meant to be equal. We're not meant to meet halfway; it's not meant to be 50/50 and that's not so I can keep the power. It's so I just want to keep the work going and I can, if I'm not careful, I can talk a bit too much.'***

In terms of professional risks, Jack's remark alerts therapists to always hold in mind the relationship differences. His expressions such as ***'paying me', 'my business', 'not meant to be 50/50'*** indicate his awareness that the relationship is not a friendship. Jack demonstrates an awareness of relational differences within the parameters of the work. Jack's repetitive use of the word **'equal',** as well as alluding to several variations of this notion, ***'not meant to meet halfway', the relationship is not '50/50'***, are indicative of the risk involved in this intimate meeting. As with most therapeutic relationships, therapists and clients meet regularly, weekly, develop a bond, therapeutic intimacy and these relational factors combined with moments of therapist self-disclosure may potentially exacerbate professional risks, taking the therapeutic relationship in another direction.

Jack's use of the words **'power'** and **'expert'** are interesting. There is a humility that comes through in his experience and expression of 'power', as he respects its presence as a necessary component to continuing the therapeutic work. Employing the word **'expert'**, more specifically his need to hold the Rogerian (1951) perspective of the client as expert, may be an indication of Jack's subconscious need to wrestle with, work with and address the inequality within the therapist-client relationship. In my view, his remark draws attention to the sensitivities involved in power dynamics within the therapist-client relationship, which are potentially caught up in the practice of therapist self-disclosure. His comment is also suggestive of the therapist's need to maintain a middle ground for themselves. Jack's attempt to **'balance'** out notions of power and **'expertise'** - and also not to create **'equality'** - may be potential admissions of the dangers and risks involved in positioning oneself in either extreme. What comes through strongly is the therapist's commitment and struggle to hold the tensions and boundaries to minimise potential professional risks to the relationship, the client, the work and their professional (and personal) self. This impression is expressed in Gabriella's comment below.

> **Gabriella said*****: 'I think as with, with someone who is already putting everything on you, yeah, like you are God or you are the doctor or you are, you know, the one who's gonna fix me or knows everything um, you know you have, for me I have to work to undo that a lot, erm, and, and so I will be very careful to say things, you know, that would reinforce that.'***

Gabriella's comment alerts therapists to the potential professional risks therapist self-disclosure may hold in relation to power dynamics. There is a sense that the therapist is aware of the client's potential need to engage in idealising the other. In this sense, the power dynamics embroiled in therapist self-disclosure is double-edged. It has the potential to allow clients to perceive their therapist as real, human and imperfect (Bugental, 1987) and simultaneously it can encourage clients to place their therapist on a pedestal, perceiving them as all-powerful (Rowan & Jacobs, 2002). It implies a professional risk to the therapeutic relationship, the work and warns of possible professional risks in reference to ethical implications. Given the uniqueness of the individual therapist's personal history, the power differentials within therapist self-disclosure could potentially trigger the therapist's unresolved narcissistic injuries leaving the client with a false sense of hope - 'you can fix me', which in turn can be regarded as mechanical, reductionistic, pathological and unethical. In this respect, the professional risks are potentially damaging for the therapeutic relationship, the work and the client. Should they indulge in such a colossal abuse of power, the therapist's self-disclosure would merely be serving their own narcissistic needs, which would imply ethical and professional dilemmas. This identifiable risk may render therapy counter-therapeutic, as the client remains hostage to an external locus of evaluation (Rogers, 1951) - as does the therapist. Furthermore, professional risks involve legal concerns, which may have implications for the therapist's ability to continue to practice. As a result, Anna's contribution below builds on the idea of therapist self-disclosure needing to be held within a 'frame' of rules, boundaries and regulations in order to minimise harm and professional risk.

> **Anna said:** ***'It can be very risky to disclose, yeah, first of all inappropriately, secondly, could be much, you know, could be, um, in terms of perpetually doing it, um, thirdly, um, irrelevant, um hugely risky, hugely risky, um, and that's why, um, the rules and regulations are set up as well, um, yeah.'***

Anna's repetition of the word **'risk'** and **'hugely risky'** mirrors the very precarious nature of this subject matter. Her response to engaging in therapist self-disclosure is suggestive of an underlying tone of personal sensitivity in this area. It may possibly indicate a past experience in which a self-disclosure had landed badly, resulting in a painful professional cost that left emotional scarring. This sense is further supported by her emphasis on **'rules'** and **'regulations'**, suggesting a mindfulness that rules and regulations offer the client protection and, for the therapist, serve as guidelines to minimise professional risk while ensuring ethical practice. Jack's contribution makes an interesting point about professional risk, as well as the benefits of non-disclosure, which can potentially be helpful to all therapists when considering the application of therapist self-disclosure in the therapist-client relationship. Even more so, it adds value to professional training standards advice to limit or discourage trainees from working with such a prospectively hazardous phenomenon before they have developed a confidence in its ethical application, which appears to only materialise with time, practice, experience and skill.

> **Jack said:** ***'The realisation that this person doesn't, isn't bound by the same rules umm, yes, I think it did very early on teach me to be very discerning and be absolutely rigidly confidential about what that person said and be very, very careful about what I say. It does also depend, and you know this, not just on the context and the relationship but if I said the setting, so in some of the more extreme places in which I have worked, in a prison, I would barely even say my name or that I was a therapist , yeah, I wouldn't even say I was a therapist, in case the prisoner who wanted to see me didn't want anybody else to know, so even the fact that I was a therapist, I sometimes had to cover up, that is quite a thing isn't it? And it was a survival tactic really, it really was, and yeah, I didn't get necessarily attacked but I did get threatened. It's just an extreme of how dangerous self-disclosure could be. So now I'm just thinking about how sometimes we are forced to be rigidly non-disclosing, but those are extreme examples.'***

Jack's contribution here provides us with an interesting albeit extreme version of 'professional' and 'personal' risks in relation to therapist self-disclosure. Jack highlights the dangers of therapist self-disclosure very clearly and also the benefits to operating a non-disclosing stance, which under the extreme conditions he describes illustrates a duty of care to the client, as well as to the self of the therapist. His emphasis, ***'that is quite a thing, isn't it?'***, is possibly indicative of the therapist's awareness of risk to safety for self and the client, and also of an added burden on the therapist in terms of wrestling with their own personal and professional sense of authenticity and congruence.

Therapists acknowledge that their self-disclosures involve assessing the client's readiness, with additional considerations around timing and decisions to disclose. The latter two points correlate with arguments put forward in the literature review, regarding engaging in therapist self-disclosure once there is a sense of a strong therapeutic relationship (which can only be fostered over time). The various schools of thought concede that early therapist self-disclosures are to be avoided, as they imply a risk to the therapeutic relationship and client. Therapists' views echo the above as they highlight the need for and importance of trust between therapist and client for therapists to venture into what can be deemed unchartered territory.

Some therapists feel 'comfortable' taking the risk of engaging in therapist self-disclosure as a means of increasing client wellbeing. Others indicate a reluctance to enter into this way of relating and being with clients, which is indicative of how the therapist's own personal experiences of self-disclosure may impact upon themself and the work. Therapist self-disclosure raises ethical concerns, as it involves decisions aimed at client beneficence and not therapist gratification (Zur, 2009). Subsequently, it is imperative that therapists take into consideration their client's presentation - emotionally, psychologically and physically - as this has implications for the client's wellbeing and ability to work with this level of intimacy within the therapeutic frame.

The Subjectivity of Therapist Self-Disclosure

Some therapists highlight caution and prefer to avoid therapist self-disclosure when working with clients who present with personality disorders and/or trauma pieces, as this has implications for the client's developmental level of engagement, as well as their ability to use the therapist as a good selfobject (Kohut, 1971). Furthermore, some therapists tend to focus on client presentation, in terms of assessing where they (client and therapist) are at in themselves and their therapeutic relationship. Assessment also involves a judgment call and trust regarding the therapist's sense of the client's readiness to go there. Overall, all therapists agree that therapist self-disclosure has the ability to powerfully impact and move therapeutic work forward. Nevertheless, therapists do acknowledge that even when therapist self-disclosure appears to be therapeutically productive, it still involves risks. These risks may render therapy counter-therapeutic, potentially blurring boundaries and interfere with the client's transference, material and process (Freud, 1912), thus potentially injuring the client and therapist. Consequently, therapists concede that therapist self-disclosure should be applied cautiously and sparingly, as it remains a vehicle that can potentially result in therapeutic breakthrough or rupture to the client, the work, the therapeutic relationship (and the disclosing therapist).

Professional Risks' Impact on Therapist Self-Disclosure and the Disclosing Therapist

Therapists demonstrate knowledge of power differentials and relationship differences in the therapist-client relationship. In order to honour as well as balance out power dynamics, it appears important for therapists that their clients experience them as another human being in the relationship. The aim is to support the client to grow in self-awareness and feel self-empowered, in terms of their experience and perspective on their presenting issue. Consequently, therapists remain vigilant and wary not to allow their clients to perceive them as all-powerful, as to do so would be suggestive of the therapist's own narcissistic injuries surfacing, while simultaneously perpetuating the client's pathological outlook on self-and-other. The view that power-play is a delicate component and requires judicious management is shared by many in the profession. Likewise, it is evident in the literature review that therapist self-disclosure can impact power dynamics, for example resulting in role reversal (Zahm, 1998). Furthermore, Audet (2011) and Gibson (2012) state that therapist self-disclosure can place certain expectations on the client. Hence, clients may feel inhibited in their process to work more authentically, demonstrate congruence (Rogers, 1951) and step forward in true self-expression (Winnicott, 1965). This attitude is further heightened if they (clients) perceive their therapist to be placing expectations on them, in terms of behaving in ways which serve the therapist's interests (Zahm, 1998). Subsequently, it may be indicative of the therapist's own wounds and unresolved past issues entering the frame and interfering with the work and the client's process, as Freud (1912) feared.

The above risks require the disclosing therapist to have a strong sense of self-awareness to be able to embrace therapist self-disclosure while simultaneously managing their countertransference feelings, experiences and embodied states. Therapists acknowledged the importance of engaging in regular self-reflexivity (Etherington, 2004) and holding an empathically curious stance (Rogers, 1951) when exploring these moments both for themselves and with their clients. A therapist's' readiness to engage at this level demonstrates their understanding of risk at various levels and their duty to be of beneficence to their clients. It highlights the therapists' ethical code to contain their own potentially narcissistic injuries from surfacing, especially as therapists, owing to their subjective and human configuration also wish and need to feel accepted by the other (and in this sense, the client) (Storr, 1990).

Chapter 11
The Emotional and Psychological Impact

This chapter aims to make transparent how therapists are emotionally and psychologically impacted by their disclosures. Here, we gain an understanding of some of the personal issues therapists face when engaged in moments of self-revelation but are by no means limited to these particular personal experiences.

> **Anna said***: **'When I was a very, very new therapist, I disclosed something, I just said, "That kinda thing happens to all of us" and it was, um, inappropriate. I regret it, um, but the client was very upset about it so I wanted to normalise it.'***

Anna's tone when speaking about this experience was rather hesitant. This reflects the impact, as her self-disclosure appears to have had a lasting effect on her, so much so that she appears momentarily uncomfortable, as a result thwarting any further exploration into her experience of that particular moment. Her repetition of the words **'very, very'** when explaining she was a new therapist at the time appears to be an attempt to rationalise what had happened for her. Recalling the experience appears to be uncomfortable, indicating that she may have felt that she had done something wrong. Anna's words, expression and embodied experience at recalling this event is indicative of the intrapsychic struggle therapists experience when engaged in therapist self-disclosure. Her experience and expression provide a heightened sense of the fragility involved in dealing with the potential ruptures this phenomenon can cause. Subsequently, Anna's experience highlights the possibility that therapist self-disclosure can cause the client to feel that their experience is not important or not in need of acknowledgment and validation, thus proving injurious. Furthermore, it brings into the frame the need for the therapist's readiness to use this phenomenon. It highlights the very real struggle that is faced by the trainee and newly qualified therapist in wrestling with therapist self-disclosure. On a personal level, Anna indicates that the experience left her with an emotional scarring that may lead her to avoid therapist self-disclosure in future. Her experience of therapist self-disclosure also appears to continue to impact her negatively, as is evident in her comment below.

> **Anna said:** ***'It doesn't often come out terribly favourably, um, really. If I can avoid doing it, I will.'***

This view of the negative impact of therapist self-disclosure on the therapist is a common feature across all participant accounts. Gabriella's experience is captured in her responses below. Thus, her self-disclosure can be categorised as involuntary and unavoidable (relating to the therapist's pregnancy).

> **Gabriella said:** ***'It had a horrible cost.'***
>
> **Gabriella said:** ***'It had a cost. Horrible, horrible.'***

Gabriella's repetitive use of the words **'cost'** and **'horrible'** is suggestive of the psychological and emotional impact therapist self-disclosure has imprinted on her. As Gabriella speaks about her experience, she demonstrates a strong sense of fear, vulnerability and acknowledges the uncertainty and struggle of attempting to keep the client, herself and the work safe. In addition to the above-mentioned negative impacts and experiences of therapist self-disclosure on the disclosing therapist, many therapists report feeling anxious, worried and vulnerable after disclosing. The anxiety and worry appear to be mostly concerned with client care. This was interesting because although the therapist sits with the psychological and emotional impact within themselves, there appears to be less of a concern for 'the self', in terms of emotional and psychological self-injury and self-care. This point is further reinforced by Miles.

> **Miles said***: **'My anxiety was that, um, that I revealed too much. Would that feel like a burden?'***

Miles' remark is an expression of the therapist's struggle with self-disclosure. The sense of 'not knowing' appears to manifest as anxiety. Miles' experience appears to have left him feeling exposed and vulnerable. In addition, his own psychological and emotional struggle has been placed on the backburner, as the client's wellbeing and the therapeutic relationship remain the central focus. The impact, as he describes it, implies a concern about role reversal, ruptures and risk to the therapeutic relationship and client. He demonstrates less concern about the impact on himself, which appears to be a secondary thought.

> **Miles said***: **'The other anxiety would have been, could this be used against me, er, in a shaming way. I don't know where that came from, probably because of the shame attached to depression.'***

Miles' response provides further insight into the therapist's process. It appears to have triggered his own experiences of depression (although resolved, there still appears to be a momentary vulnerability). This notion of vulnerability is further expressed in Miles' use of the word **'shame'.** Many therapists acknowledge that moments of therapist self-disclosure can reactivate past or current traumas, emotional and developmental deficits within themselves, thus alluding to the power of self-disclosure and the vulnerability it exposes due to 'not knowing' its impact until it happens. Nevertheless, notwithstanding the negative impact therapist self-disclosure can have on the personal self of the disclosing therapist, most concur with its therapeutic value to move the work forward and deepen the connection between therapist and client. Consequently, therapists are able to recall moments in which their disclosures resulted in a positive impact.

> **Anna said*: 'So I guess it, um, I guess it showed the disclosure could help the client feel a bit more connected to you.'***
>
> **Cristina said: *'The impact of me was to show vulnerability in a person who would understand in the same way. I feel the patient felt understood by me.'***

Both Anna and Cristina's accounts acknowledge the positive impact therapist self-disclosure holds for the client, the work and the therapeutic relationship. Therapist self-disclosure appears to strengthen the bond and gives the client a 'felt sense' that the therapist understands and empathises with their struggle. Interestingly, Cristina's quote subtly points to the duality of this phenomenon as she places her own subjectivity in the frame. This demonstrates the therapist's very real human need to also feel met and accepted by their client (Storr, 1990). To my mind, her response signifies the importance of both subjectivities needing to be met in the service of healing for the client - which may also heal parts of the therapist. There is a sense that they (clients) are not alone. This notion is further corroborated below by Jack.

> **Jack said*: 'I certainly found that in prison the guys needed to see recognition when they talk about, okay, they were criminals and they were found guilty, but when they talk about the horrors of incarceration, they needed to see that you felt something, that's my belief. Again nothing dramatic, but just a sense of compassion, something to connect, that you felt something for them.'***

Jack emphasises connection with the other, a need for the client to 'feel felt' and for the therapist to really see their current situation and plight in being incarcerated. This extreme context highlights what most clients (and therapists) yearn for – acceptance, even on a very human level. Jack's experience is demonstrative of therapist self-disclosure conveying compassion and recognising the humanity within the individual. This interplay, in turn, allows for connection, movement and growth within the intersubjective meeting (Stolorow et al, 1987). What comes through strongly is that although the therapist's self-disclosures are primarily intended to be of benefit for their clients, they also acknowledge the positive impact on themselves.

> **Cristina said***: 'So it made me feel more humble in that moment... that I was able to share it and it didn't... it wasn't dropped in the same way as their experience wasn't dropped.'*

There is a sense here that, in moments of therapist self-disclosure, the therapist also needs to know that they are being accepted as a fellow human being, removed from the pedestal that some clients place them on and yet still operating within the boundaries of an asymmetrical relationship. In my view, therapist self-disclosure is a valuable and useful therapeutic tool and should always be cautiously applied, as the impact of 'not knowing' how it will be received has significant implications for client wellbeing, the therapeutic relationship, professionalism and therapist self-care. It is clear that therapists hold positive and negative experiences and impacts in relation to their self-disclosures. Previous research affirms that, in most cases, therapist self-disclosure is viewed positively by clients (Audet, 2011, Knox et al, 1997) and this position correlates with therapist accounts. Therapists acknowledge that these positive experiences often left them feeling vulnerable.

Gibson (2012) and Zahm's (1998) respective contributions remind us of the sensitivities involving power-play and that negative consequences reportedly left clients feeling resentful and distrusting of their therapist (Audet, 2001; Gibson, 2012). Negative experiences related to therapist self-disclosure reportedly intensified the therapist's sense of their vulnerability and fragility. They often left a lasting impression on the disclosing therapist, including a heightened sense of anxiety and worry.

Consequently, negative experiences of therapist self-disclosure often lead therapists to attempt to avoid it. These intensely vulnerable and anxiety provoking moments raise issues around the therapist's perceived sense of emotional safety for self (and by implication the client). Despite this awareness, there still appears to be consensus among therapists to focus on the emotional, psychological and physical safety of their clients, arguably due to the ethical implications of holding the client's wellbeing as central and paramount. This perceived imbalance highlights the disparity between ethics and practice and amplifies issues involving therapist self-care.

Therapists do affirm that, at times, it is necessary to take the risk of self-revelation, as the benefits to the client far outweigh the risks to the therapeutic relationship, the work and the therapist. In line with Ehrenberg's (1995) view, many therapists agree that therapist self-disclosure is a necessary part of the therapeutic work. Furthermore, therapist accounts' correlate with the study carried out by Knox et al (1997), thus recognising that therapist self-disclosure is experienced as helpful by the client and results in a deeper connection between therapist and client. Therapist self-disclosure allowed for more moments of authentic engagement (Rogers, 1951) within the intersubjective meeting (Stolorow et al, 1987). It is important to note that therapists' do acknowledge the uneasiness they feel when embroiled in these moments. Yet, their conviction of duty and care towards their clients, coupled with their accountability to their profession and ethics, provides them with the courage to take these risks in the service of healing for their clients.

Chapter 12
Influences of power, motivation and the shadow

Here, we pay close attention to the influence of power, motivation and the shadow in respect of these variables' entanglement with this phenomenon. Therapists in general, recognise the power differentials that exist within this phenomenon. Consequently, this awareness points to a need for therapists to be very careful in their moment-to-moment assessment of therapist self-disclosure, as the power-play can go either way. Henceforth, it feels important for therapists to remain open to self-reflexivity whilst assessing their motivations behind therapist self-disclosure.

> **Cristina said: *'Who is it for? Is it for the person who wants to, feels wants to share something that is important for it to be out there, or, um, is it for the other person?'***

Cristina's comment is suggestive of the rigorous assessment process therapists engage in when grappling with the decision to self-disclose. Her response also indicates her awareness of accountability, ethical concerns and the need to always use self-disclosure as a means of therapeutic benefit for the client. Cristina goes on to address the sometimes overt, sometimes subtle power dynamics involved in therapist self-disclosure, which is evident in the following comment below.

> **Cristina said:** ***'You don't want too many elements of your own self-disclosure on the painting. Ideally, you want to have the, the patient's self-disclosure there on the painting, because that's what they take home with them, but it's also nice to have a few colours in there from the therapist.'***

Her description of self-disclosure as an interplay of artistic expression is interesting. Her analogy conjures up a picture of the client leaving the therapy space with their own artwork, their own sense of authority, authenticity and autonomy, which has been guided and empathically held by the therapist. This is illustrated in her phrase '***but it's also nice to have a few colours in there from the therapist***'. Cristina acknowledges the power that is born out of therapist self-disclosure.

> **Cristina said:** ***'I think real connection happens and what you do with it is your call. Erm, it's an opportunity. It's almost like a golden opportunity for something big to happen, if you choose to disclose something.'***

The power element is ambiguous in that therapist self-disclosure comes with the possibility of 'not knowing' the outcome until it happens. Simultaneously, there is a sense that the therapist holds the power. This is evident in her phrase ***'what you do with it is your call'***. Anna's response highlights power relations within the therapeutic relationship and, by implication, 'therapist self-disclosure'.

> **Anna said:** ***'I have to be very careful because the client doesn't want to be, er, usurped in importance in their, um, in the therapy.'***

Anna's remark points to how power in relation to therapist self-disclosure can shift the focus away from the client and onto the therapist, thus rendering the therapeutic relationship and work counter-therapeutic. She alerts the reader to further risks: the possibility of reinforcing the client's emotional injuries and developmental deficits regarding being seen, heard and feeling that they matter. This point is further explored in the comments below.

> **Gabriella said:** ***'People are coming to see you, but for help, they want help and, um, you already have an idealised version of this, this person knows what's wrong with me or knows how, how to fix me. So if you occupy that position you, you know, in a way you become like a tyrant or like a, um, like an almighty (laugh) figure... Therapist in the same line as Jesus (laugh) and (laugh) that is what you know, that is something I strongly feel, um, at least in my practice, that's not the chair I want to occupy and it's difficult because you might even sometimes have this narcissistic side; illusions, that you are because um all these people come to you for help.'***

> **Gabriella said:** ***'I think as with someone who is already putting everything on you, yeah, like you are God or you are the doctor or you are, you know, the one who's gonna fix me or knows everything, um, you know you have to, for me, I have to work to undo that a lot erm, and so I will be very careful to say things, you know, that would reinforce that.'***

Gabriella's wariness of the power dynamics caught up in therapist self-disclosure clearly allude to the clients' perception and expectations of the therapist, as well as providing a flavour of the shadow side of therapist self-disclosure. Gabriella's experience warns of how therapist self-disclosure can be transferentially played out with clients idealising their therapists. This can further heighten the possibility of risk if the therapist has unresolved narcissistic traits that they continue to be unaware of. Gabriella's use of words such as ***'fix me'***, the therapist as

'God', ***'Jesus'***, the ***'Almighty'***, a ***'tyrant'*** and ***'doctor'*** highlight the dangers regarding power dynamics within the therapist-client relationship when therapist self-disclosures are made. Her reference to the therapist's possible ***'narcissistic illusions'*** also highlights potential avenues in which therapists can become hooked into feeding their own unresolved issues. These concerns are shared by other therapists, as is evident in the following remark.

> **Miles said:** ***'I think this was the shadow side of self-disclosure. If you didn't get witnessed and seen enough as a child yourself, adolescent, teenager, young person, young man, young woman, there could be, the shadow side of disclosure, personal piece, you could want to share stuff because you want to be seen... And, of course, if you did, if you weren't seen enough as a child, adolescent, or a person, then you could get hooked too quickly to start sharing stuff, which you're thinking with all good intent is for the client, but actually it's for you.'***

Miles names the shadow as a motivational influence in therapist self-disclosure. He alerts the therapist to be mindful of their own personal process as their own past injuries may trigger the need to self-disclose. Miles' comment illustrates a cautionary approach to the therapist's use of self-disclosure. His comment goes on to highlight the need for therapists to pay attention to their own self-care, so that what they choose to share remains therapeutically appropriate and productive for their clients, while allowing the therapists to work with their shadow influences within the appropriate avenues of personal therapy, supervision, peer supervision and self-reflexivity.

Although Miles highlights the shadow side of therapist self-disclosure, he adopts an integrative stance in this respect, as he says: ***'I think sometimes revealing yourself can take you out of the ivory tower, like some clients put us transferentially.'*** His comment attempts to address the power dynamics and use of therapist self-disclosure within this asymmetrical relationship. In addition, his response emphasises the need for therapists to help clients see them as another human being in the service of healing, when they are ready to do so. Anna's narrative makes clear how moments of therapist self-disclosure have interfered with the power dynamics within the therapist-client relationship while also revealing its personal impact upon her and can be seen in her response below.

> **Anna said:** ***'I've been, er, disempowered and have to, had to answer it even though I don't want to and they might feel sorry for me or I might have lost some of my gravitas or they might start to judge me.'***

On a personal level, Anna's self-esteem as a therapist is very much interlinked with how her clients may perceive her. My sense is that a potential impact of the power-play involved in therapist self-disclosure centres around her fear of judgment and sympathy from her clients. This is reflected in her choice of words such as ***'judge'*** and ***'feel sorry for me'***. Anna's narrative echoes a strong sense of the vulnerability experienced by the disclosing therapist, which is further emphasised in her comment below.

> **Anna says:** ***'I felt disempowered.'***

This sense of the therapist feeling powerless is further illuminated in Anna's repetition of this theme later in our interview. This made me wonder about her vulnerability around her self-esteem when in the midst of a disclosure, as Anna admitted that her regular job is not very high-powered. Therefore, I recognise her sensitivity in relation to power differentials and how they may impact her on a personal level. Following on, Jack's comment emphasises the therapists' wariness when contemplating self-revelation.

> **Jack said:** ***'The realisation that this person doesn't, isn't bound by the same rules, um, yes, I think it did very early on teach me to be very discerning and it's absolutely rigidly confidential about what that person said and be very, very careful about what I say.'***

The above response demonstrates Jack's awareness of power differentials within the therapeutic relationship. His comment ***'this person isn't bound by the same rules'*** is indicative of his perception that whatever he chooses to share can be repeated outside of the therapeutic space. Jack's response offers evidence of the therapist's vulnerability and powerlessness in relation to what they share with their clients. In my view, Jack's narrative offers an interesting perspective, in view of therapist self-disclosure and power-play, and it is also evident in his response below.

> **Jack said:** ***'So I quite like the fact that you can say anything and that I can never ever tell anyone. It's a kind of (long pause) the, the sort of safety vacuum... I mustn't and I wouldn't ever tell anybody. So I think I quite like the feeling that your secrets are safe with me... Yeah, safe and it all stays in this room and no one will ever know we've had this conversation.'***

Jack's position here does suggest the power imbalance favours the therapist. Although his understanding of power does not specifically involve therapist self-disclosure in this instance, his approach offers food for thought as his use of power in this respect feels appropriate. In his eyes, the power balance is weighed in favour for the benefit and protection of the client and the client's material. His repetitive use of words such as ***'safety'*** and ***'safe'*** highlight his need to keep the space safe for the client. Following on, this notion of 'safety' leaves me wondering if there is a possibility, perhaps a subconscious realisation that the space was not a place of safety for the therapist.

In general, therapists acknowledge the delicate nature of power-play. the importance of holding an awareness of power differentials, their motivational force behind self-disclosure and the potential shadow side of therapist self-disclosure. This awareness further leads therapists to work towards remaining in a continuous state of assessment, which is captured in Cristina's response ***'It feels freakin exhausting.'*** Within this frame, there also exists professional and ethical accountability as well as clinical implications. What is clear is that in their pursuit to be of beneficence to their clients', therapists generally wish to ethically, clinically and therapeutically honour power differentials within this asymmetrical relationship. Therapists' commitment to work through and understand potential power struggles, if and when they arise, from a place of empathic curiosity and exploration for both self-and-other, is indicative of ethical considerations. Holding in mind this sensitivity supports therapists to allow themselves to be used as a good selfobject (Kohut, 1971) in the transference and therapeutic relationship. Subsequently, clients may not necessarily feel disempowered but instead experience their story, trauma and hurt being acknowledged, validated and witnessed (Miller, 1995), thus potentially resulting in a 'corrective emotional experience' (Alexander, 1961).

Power-play as an extension of therapist self-disclosure can encompass a darker side – the shadow. This sentiment is acknowledged and shared by all therapists. However, it is important to acknowledge that although the shadow is known for holding our darker content and qualities, it also holds many hidden parts that are not necessarily destructive. Jung's (1993) notion of the shadow is a useful concept for therapists to consider when contemplating a disclosure and exploring their motivational force. Jung (1993) alerts the therapist to embrace, work with and familiarise themselves with their shadow parts. Therapists' attempts to hold a conscious awareness of this unconscious part ensures that the work, the therapeutic relationship, the client's material and the client's process are not usurped or interfered with. Therapists do acknowledge the power self-revelation has to potentially trigger their own narcissistic or unresolved injuries/needs. In this respect, many therapists' emphasis the need to foster emotional robustness so that they are more able to own and manage their shadow parts. I make an integrative link with holding in mind how power, motivation and shadow parts can also entail risk. Furthermore, therapists concede that the therapist's readiness to use self-disclosure involves experience and skill, which in turn is strongly linked with therapist robustness. Consequently, the therapist's willingness and accountability to 'deal with their own demons' allows the therapeutic space (in which therapist self-disclosures manifest) to remain emotionally safe, and therapeutically and clinically productive for the client and the client's material.

Therapists appear to remain cognisant of ethical implications and accountability, as they acknowledge the possibility of the shadow side of therapist self-disclosure as a motivational force aimed at indulging the therapist's needs. In view of power differentials, there is consensus among therapists for the need to therapeutically cross idealising transactions when appropriate, in two-person psychology/intersubjective meeting (Stark, 2000; Stolorow et al, 1987), with a more authentic, humanity-based and humble presence. This way, clients perceive their therapist as real, imperfect and fallible (Bugental, 1987). In contrast, it is also necessary to honour the dubious quality 'power' holds within the therapeutic frame as there is a very real and strong sense of hurt that can be manifest when operating the delicate notion of 'power'. In this sense, what comes through strongly for the therapist is the very fragile sense of feeling disempowered and emotionally injured in moments of therapist self-disclosure. This sensitivity makes me wonder about the very careful 'workings' of the power dynamic, in terms of its potential to re-awaken the therapist's past emotional injuries and unresolved material. Consequently, this fragility exists in all human beings (therapists are not exempt), and therefore self-disclosure poses a risk of huge cost to the therapist's vulnerable and emotional self - their self-esteem, self-worth and self-value.

In relation to power differentials, Jack's earlier response regarding ***'power dynamics'*** places a unique spin on the notion of 'power' pertaining to therapist self-disclosure - that the keeping of secrets and keeping secrets safe embodies a sense of power. Hence, ethical and professional adherence to the boundary of client confidentiality is a 'power' held by the therapist and its impact in this respect is afforded the client and not the therapist. The thought process regarding 'power', in this respect, is interesting – power, in this respect allows the therapist to be of benefit and service to the client in a protective manner. Hence, power is not viewed as a tool that could potentially place the therapist in the position of being seen as expert. On the one hand, owing to the asymmetrical composition of the therapist-client relationship, I acknowledge that most therapists may concur that the notion of client confidentiality is an extension of 'power' and on the other hand 'power' as embodied within a therapist's self-disclosure is a qualitatively different experience, one which often leaves therapists feeling exposed, vulnerable and powerless over their shared disclosures.

Chapter 13
Vulnerability and Humanity as Integral to the Self of the Therapist and the Wounded Healer

Now we explore the therapist's use of self in relation to therapist self-disclosure. This area, the vulnerability and humanity of the therapist in relation to therapist self-disclosure, takes a deeper look at how therapists self-disclosures shared with their clients impact upon them personally. It is important to note that the content uncovered serves to provide a snapshot of the personal experience and impact therapist self-disclosure has on the disclosing therapist. Furthermore, in the interest of showcasing this intense subject matter, I feel compelled to add that all therapist accounts included in this chapter merely aim to capture this process and are by no means exhaustive in terms of the material that can be manifest. Moreover, the vulnerability and humanity experienced by the disclosing therapist can show itself in many ways, both consciously and subconsciously. Sometimes, the therapist's exposure to their own vulnerability is experienced as so extremely raw and fragile that it can be missed or dismissed.

> **Cristina said:** ***'It's quite powerful when you think about talking about vulnerability. It's something powerful behind a word that can create a lot of anxiety and stress. That's why I feel it's fear and strength together.'***

Cristina's comment alerts the reader to the paradox encompassed within the notion of 'vulnerability'. Her choice of words **'powerful'**, **'vulnerability'**, **'fear'** and **'strength'** all convey a sense of the potential turmoil the disclosing therapist is left to grapple with after sharing their disclosure with a client. Moreover, in these moments, the triggering of their own anxieties, self-doubts and past emotional injuries may have implications for their professional and ethical practice, as well as self-care. Her repetition of the word **'powerful'** lends weight to the notion of how therapist self-disclosure can be experienced as quite evocative and potentially traumatising for the therapist. This aspect of therapist self-disclosure is suggestive of an experience in which the therapist is left feeling exposed - to the client and to themselves. There is an element of the therapist needing to be protective over themselves and their vulnerabilities, and this notion is further corroborated in Cristina's commentary that follows when she talks about her client disclosing his fear, worry and anxiety about spending Christmas on his own.

> **Cristina said:** ***'Perhaps it brought something for me in that moment I wanted to dismiss as well, so I guess I did not want to disclose perhaps my feelings, that I was going to be away from my family. I hadn't, which I said, but even for me, it was something more than that. I would be away from my family, I didn't have any plans, I was probably going to spend Christmas on my own, and this realisation already evoked anxiety and stress, so I dismissed it.'***

Cristina's experience of vulnerability in relation to therapist self-disclosure can also be viewed as projective identification. Her experience is indicative of the subconscious experience of the parallel process that sometimes operates between therapist and client. It appears that the therapist experienced a very real intrapsychic conflict between disclosure and non-disclosure. Cristina went on to acknowledge the anxiety and stress she experienced in the moment. Given the fragility experienced by both parties, there is a sense that the therapist is careful not to allow her countertransference feelings and her personal piece to usurp her client's experience. Her non-disclosure may be suggestive of her need to be protective of her vulnerabilities and unresolved material, which needs further exploration outside of the therapist-client relationship while simultaneously being there for her client.

Consequently, non-disclosure may also be interpreted as an attempt to contain and hold the client's experience. Cristina's response feels symptomatic of Ehrenberg's (1995) notion that to do nothing in these moments is just as dangerous as disclosing. Hence, the impact of leaving her with feelings of regret that she had missed her client in that moment while dismissing her own feelings. Later, Cristina confirms this sense of regret with her admission ***'also I missed my own vulnerability'.*** This sense of the therapist's vulnerability and humanity when disclosing to clients is further amplified by Miles' reflections on his experience of self-disclosure.

> **Miles said:** ***'With that, there are ramifications. There come costs, maybe to your family, your culture, your religion, your relationship.'***

Miles' experience of vulnerability alerts the reader to the dangers and risks involved for the disclosing therapist. His use of the word **'ramifications'** evokes a sense of danger, which he acknowledges can not only penetrate and damage the therapeutic relationship, but also severely jeopardise the therapist in a very personal way – their culture, religion, family, the therapist's self. Miles' view of his vulnerability is further reinforced in the following comment, in which he names his experience as anxiety.

> **Miles said:** ***'I was quite anxious afterwards, because then I realised you'd given a part of yourself away, and she could do whatever she wants with it.'***

Miles is referring to the potential powerlessness a therapist can experience after disclosing, coupled with very intense emotional and embodied experiences. These intense experiences are shared by many if not all therapists. This sentiment is reiterated in Gabriella's remark, which speaks of her vulnerability at being pregnant and having to work with a client whose partner indirectly threatened her safety and that of her child.

> **Gabriella said:** ***'So that was, er, extremely hard and it had a huge cost in many ways because it went on for some time. And it did take me to a place of quite, quite, of, of, fear and, I, yeah, and you know, that had to do with, with past experiences, in the environment and where I grew up. It was difficult to manage in terms of, okay, I'm feeling really scared and it's bringing up all these things from, from my past... I can see in my reactions or in, or in my, you know, being kinda like a little paranoid in the streets.***
>
> ***'I supervised a lot and talked a lot with my supervisor and, mmm, but because, for me, the need not to drop my patient was really important as well, and I really thought that if we, we were able to go through it together, in a way, that meant we were both safe and the work was safe, cos it was an attempt to disrupt the work, really, what, what my client's partner was doing and, you know, I took the risk of understanding it that way and think, okay, I don't think he's going to call me or my child, or you know, but I took precautions.'***

Gabriella's vulnerabilities were clearly very much in the fore of her experience. Her use of words such as **'risk', 'paranoid', 'scared'** all illustrate the emotional and psychological turmoil the therapist experiences when feeling vulnerable. Recalling this episode appears to momentarily dysregulate Gabriella, which is evident in her speech. There is a limbic resonance/regulation (Schore, 2005) that comes out as she speaks of her experience, in terms of her repetition of words such as **'quite', 'in', 'we' and 'what'**, which adds to her experience of fear and vulnerability.

I wondered if perhaps recalling her experience made her feel vulnerable and that perhaps her rhythmic manner of speaking may have been an attempt to regulate her emotional self. These intense emotions appear to be balanced out with the need to keep the therapist, client and work safe. Her mention of the word **'precautions'** resonates with a sense of possible danger, concerns about safety and gives the impression of needing to be hypervigilant or on high alert – traits that may be indicative of her experience possibly mirroring a trauma response. As with other therapist accounts, there was an overwhelming need to '*be there*' for her client. To my mind, the therapist's duty of care to their client appears to hold more significance than their duty of care to themself, even in the face of real danger. This is an interesting development, because it can be suggestive of the therapist's need to remain professional, ethical and '*be there*' for their client at the expense of self-care and '*being there*' for themselves. Consequently, it has implications for therapist self-care. This point is further elaborated on by Jack's experience of vulnerability and the need to hold a non-disclosing stance.

> **Jack said:** ***'My brother died not, not that long ago, on a Monday and I was due in here on the Tuesday to see six or seven people in a row, and I found it easier to come in and keep those appointments than move all those people, because I didn't know what I would tell them. I couldn't imagine saying something so awful has happened, I can't keep the appointment tomorrow. I couldn't lie about having the flu (pause). Does it make any sense? I just found it easier to turn up and act normally for 50 minutes and then there was 10 minutes of panic mode before I see the next client. I wasn't trying to be a hero, I just didn't know how to cancel them. I'm just saying that I could contain myself and think in the moment this is who I am and this is what I'm doing and the other stuff is, is too huge to process so I'd rather go to work because there I have these seven people lined up, that's what I chose to do. I think it was all right, I spoke to another therapist about it***

> ***and she'd done something similar and she said, actually, looking back, I think really what we should do is take a few days or weeks off, get on with the horrors of grieving but I couldn't agree. All I could do was turn up and do the stuff, yeah.'***

Jack's narrative exposes the rawness and the robustness that therapists must be in possession of to work with their clients' wounds while simultaneously keeping their own traumas and injuries contained. The work itself and the need to *be there* for their clients unconditionally proves to be an important obligation therapists employ, which potentially supports and contains them while in the throes of danger and tragedy. In this respect, Jack's contribution echoes Gabriella's sense of needing to be protective of the therapist's self and '*be there*' for their client. There is still a sense that, in these moments of vulnerability, a possibly subconscious need emerges on the part of the therapist to be dismissive of their own self-care (a theme shared by many therapists) and focus their efforts on remaining duty-bound to their client's well-being. To my mind, this may be the therapist's protective instinct, their defence mechanism supporting them to contain their material. However, it is important to note that this duty-bound 'work ethic' raises ethical concerns in relation to the therapist's self-care.

Following on, Anna's contribution reveals the therapist's vulnerability of feeling exposed when faced with an accidental self-disclosure.

> **Anna said: *'I felt quite naked that he could see me in a different environment, so I felt very, erm, stripped of my therapeutic mask if you can, therapeutic persona in that environment.'***

Anna's experience of vulnerability links with the notion of exposure, hence her remark, ***'I felt naked.'*** There is a sense of the therapist wanting to appear professional and holding onto her power. This image is eclipsed by her experience of the mask falling off, leaving the other her, perhaps the human being - her true self - exposed (Winnicott, 1965). There is also a sense of this human self possibly interfering with the transference. On another level, it can also be interpreted as the therapist's own intrapsychic conflicts regarding her authenticity being unwillingly invited into the therapeutic frame. Anna's experience of feeling vulnerable in the moment of therapist self-disclosure is also evident in her next comment.

> **Anna said:** ***'Er, bit of dread to be honest (nervous laugh), um, a bit of dread because, er, (pause) er, and vulnerability. I really don't want to be that vulnerable in front of my clients.'***

Anna repeats the word **'dread'** in relation to self-disclosure and this may be suggestive of her inclination to avoid therapist self-disclosure, as it may be experienced as disempowering or an attempt to peel off the professional mask/persona. There is a strong impression here of her need for her clients to see her as a therapist rather than as a human being, at times. This protective mechanism may be indicative of the therapist's own struggle to be seen as a fellow human being and feel 'comfortable' basking in her own authenticity. There is also an element of the therapist's exposed vulnerabilities potentially becoming disruptive to the therapeutic relationship, as it may result in role reversal with clients emotionally holding (Winnicott, 1965) their therapist.

Cristina supports the theory that the therapist and client need to meet intersubjectively (Stolorow et al, 1987). Thus, both therapist and client need to be engaged in an interactive two-way interpersonal process (Siegel 1999) for the work to happen and for the client to progress. Given this book's focus, I argue that these interactive ways of relating also progress the therapist. I am reminded of Casement's (1990) contribution, which demonstrates the therapist's humility and humanity as he contends that we (therapists) are in the process of learning as much from the patient as they are learning from us. The following comments provided by therapists are illustrative of the need for connection within the therapist-client relationship and demonstrate how therapist self-disclosure can be a powerful tool in this respect.

> **Cristina said:** ***'I also feel like there needs to be a human sitting opposite them, not just a mirror... I would like to think there is a human being interested in me rather than someone who is sort of giving technique or intervention, not being in a particular way, that I would find very wooden and alienated, alienating.'***

Jack, Miles and Gabriella's understanding of the vulnerability and humanity encompassed in therapist self-disclosure further emphasises the above-mentioned point.

> **Jack said:** ***'I hope they think, though (pause) he's had to deal with challenges too, he's an ordinary bloke like me, um, just because you're a therapist doesn't mean that your life is easy to manage (pause). I think that might just help them realise that so much of life is random and whatever you're doing, bad things will happen and it's how we manage those bad things really, so perhaps they think, I hope they think, "Oh, he always seems okay and yet, there have been those examples of difficult times having to be coped with.'***
>
> **Gabriella said:** ***'A sense of being there, yeah, of there's something human and maybe the self-disclosure will be more of you showing, you know, showing how human you are.'***
>
> **Miles said:** ***'When you disclose, you, in their eyes, you join the human race.'***

Jack, Miles and Gabriella give us more of a sense of the therapist's need to themselves be seen as imperfect, fallible and human (Bugental, 1987) - in a sense, breaking the transference and dispelling the idealising piece contained within it. There is a need for the therapist to be perceived as another human being joining the client in the service of healing yet honouring the asymmetry existing within the therapeutic relationship.

Displaying elements of humanity through therapist self-disclosure can also be viewed as a very necessary therapeutic manoeuvre intended to support the development of the 'real relationship' (Clarkson, 1995), where both client and therapist can meet holding their authenticity (Rogers, 1951) within the mutuality of the exchange. Anna's response illustrates a slight shift in favour of protecting the vulnerability of the therapist as she discusses the notion of discussing therapist self-disclosure and recognises that actively engaging in these discussions is, in itself, a form of self-disclosure.

> **Anna said:** ***'I suppose you could ask something about the disclosure procedure as I'm disclosing, aren't I, at the moment? And whether or not there would be anything that would stop me disclosing to you.***
>
> ***'Um, that would be one interesting thing, because the disclosure that I regretted, I wouldn't even put into words, um, because I was embarrassed, I was naïve. It did affect the therapy probably, but it was my first client, so I guess, is there disclosure about disclosure (laugh)? Even as I'm speaking in the interview, you're thinking do I need to disclose cos obviously there's another side to conducting the interview and not to say too much or too little, so there really is a real disclosure process, perhaps there's a parallel process going on here, which is interesting, so yeah, it is quite vulnerable, yeah.'***

Anna's narrative outlines the caution and wariness invoked by therapist self-disclosure. Her assessment on whether to self-disclose or not involves her sense of accountability to her profession, her insurance, UKCP, her client's welfare and her own. Her response gives us an indication of how the therapist's vulnerabilities are experienced on multi-levels. Her use of words such as **'embarrassed'** and **'naive'** suggests that her experience of being vulnerable in the midst of therapist self-disclosure and also in this interview remains very much enmeshed within her core and evokes an uncomfortable embodied experience of this phenomenon. Moreover, it is important to hold that this notion of vulnerability and humanity is not confined to this particular theme – the vulnerability and humanity of the disclosing therapist - as its echo infiltrates aspects of areas previously discussed (such as the emotional and psychological self of the therapist, power, motivation and the shadow). This notion, vulnerability and humanity is also dominant in the subject matter pertaining to the Therapist as a 'Wounded Healer'.

Therapists concede that their disclosures leave them feeling exposed and vulnerable, as well as allowing their humanity to be more fully present in these moments. While therapists hold in mind a broad range of 'assessment criteria', albeit based on their personal and unique make-up, they also acknowledge the very personal impact their disclosures have on *them*. One therapist bravely shared their disclosure of depression to demonstrate to his client that it may be possible to work through a mental health condition. This disclosure offered the client a sense of hope. In contrast, the therapist's disclosure evoked in himself a sense of panic, anxiety and shame. I believe these latter impacts experienced by the therapist to be indicative of the therapists' humanity and vulnerability entering the frame. Furthermore, these impacts resonate with the discussion regarding the emotional and psychological impact of therapist self-disclosure.

For some therapists, the experience of therapist self-disclosure (even when unavoidable) leaves a lasting impact regarding their personal safety, the safety of their family and their client. Again, this links with the human fragility, which can leave the therapist feeling paranoid and fearful. Furthermore, it can re-awaken past developmental traumas. It is argued that therapists in general need to be in possession of 'good enough' (Winnicott, 1965) emotional robustness (which I maintain is very much a necessity when in the realm of therapist self-disclosure). Thus, it appears that therapists are willing to put themselves in a position of vulnerability and fragility while holding their past wounds and hurts, and using this shared wound as a strength. In this way, it can be supposed that perhaps, they support both themselves and their respective clients to reach a point of resolve and real safety - physically, emotionally and psychologically.

Additionally, what is made transparent is the idea that therapists, just like their clients, are in the process of trying to understand, integrate and work with their own material. Sometimes, this happens within the two-way interpersonal process. Perhaps therapist self-disclosure may also support clients (and therapists) to work through their own 'broken line of being' (Winnicott, 1965). Therapists stepping forward in the 'uncomfortability' of their own vulnerabilities, fragilities, authenticity - and as fellow human beings - validate the human need to share with the other (the client) the hope and possibility of coping and managing trauma, hurt, emotional and psychological disturbances in healthier ways. Adopting an integrative stance where therapists hold the luminosity and the shadow supports clients to hold a both/and position of their realities, in which 'good' and 'bad' in the self can co-exist and be embraced, understood, accepted, empathically held and integrated. Nevertheless, therapists continue to remain heavily bridled to the notion that therapist self-disclosure still requires therapists to be clear as to their decisions to disclose. Subsequently, this therapeutic tool remains a vehicle for client benefit and not an opportunity for therapist self-gratification, blurring of boundaries or over-identification with the clients' experience and material (Maroda, 1990).

Moreover, the impression of therapist self-disclosure being both helpful and unhelpful for clients also attests to the personal impact on the therapist. This is especially pertinent when the **'therapist's mask slips off'** and exposes their humanity and vulnerability. This can impact the therapist's sense of self and their self-esteem. It may cause moments of self-doubt regarding the therapist's professional self (and by implication, their personal self), the therapeutic work, the therapeutic relationship and how therapists (in these very delicate and sensitive moments) perceive their clients to be experiencing them. The vulnerability and humanity of the therapist's self in moments of therapist self-disclosure requires therapists to manage their countertransference feelings and hold the boundaries through awareness of 'what is their stuff' and what belongs to the other (the client). This careful, conscious tuning into self-and-other allows the therapist to make more emotional and psychological space available for therapeutic work with their clients and by implication via self-care practises it also honours the work therapists to do on themselves.

The Therapist as a 'Wounded Healer'

Here, we explore the therapists' use of self-disclosure and incorporate their vulnerability and humanity within their humble pursuit as wounded healers in the service of healing. The following comments really draw out the emotional impact on the therapist when self-disclosing to their client. They give a sense of the therapist being reminded of their own vulnerabilities, as well as their own unresolved wounds. Below Cristina's commentary illustrates theses vulnerabilities.

> **Cristina said:** ***'I think what's costly is when you agree with the patient inside of your mind, and you're thinking to yourself, God, yeah, I know exactly what you mean, and in the moment, it brings me back to my own space, it brings me back to my own fears, or my own anxieties.'***
>
> ***'So that was quite costly in the sense that, yes, we met, but also it brought up my own fears and my own anxieties, so there was a meeting. But there was also something that is quite costly for me in a sense. It brings me back to my own sense of, you know, I understand you and I also did not want to be in that position... or maybe I am, so you know, it brings you back to those questions in your own mind.'***
>
> ***'So I think the cost for me is that it takes me away from the therapy room for a bit, until I regroup myself and my thoughts, and try to use that experience as an empathy.'***
>
> ***'The cost for me is that it brings certain things that I know I need to address, you know, it just brings a box into my check list I need to work on outside of the room, and use it empathically rather than in an alienating kind of sense, where I'm off, out the room, I've left you to it because I'm, I'm next door, um, so I guess the cost for me is that it brings certain things that I know I need to address. It***

> ***touches something that is quite personal and quite sensitive.'***
>
> ***'So, there is a cost both for the patient in that I have checked out for a bit and when I check out, I go into a little bit of a bubble, but it's just for a few minutes, I know I'm coming back. It also shows , you know, no therapist has ever resolved everything in their lives. It can be quite painful to know that not everything in your life had been resolved (laughs).***
>
> ***'You still have open wounds, it can be quite painful. It is also very painful to see, particularly you also need to be in check with what is going on in the moment.'***

Cristina's narrative details her experience of moments when therapist self-disclosure reminded her of her own wounds. She refers to the cost involved for herself, the client and the work, acknowledging that in those very intrapsychic moments, there is a need for the therapist to hold themselves, remain emotionally robust and on occasions this means briefly dissociating from the experience as a protective mechanism.

There is a sense that Cristina accepts that this cost is a necessary 'evil', in that it keeps the client and the therapist safe, so that the work can continue. Her comment conveys her empathy and emotional response to the client and the work. It also suggests that she is acknowledging her humanness, vulnerabilities and position as a wounded healer. Her repetitive use of the words **'pain'** and **'painful'** are indicative of the rawness she experiences when being faced with the mirror reflecting back her own wounds. These costly wounding experiences conjure up deep-seated emotion and hurt that maybe lay dormant as the vulnerability of these wounds feel too overwhelming to touch. Cristina goes on to reveal more of the emotional impact on her.

> **Cristina said:** ***'I saw her checking my wedding finger, for instance too, cos I don't think she's ever done that, that, so that broke me a little bit.'***

Her comment demonstrates her need to hold her wounds and contain her countertransferential feelings and experience. It describes an attempt to be there for her client, providing emotional holding (Winnicott, 1965) and a safe, secure base (Bowlby, 1998) while at the same time putting on the brakes (Rothschild, 2003), to avoid flooding the client and taking anything away from the client's experience or their (client's) right to be acknowledged, witnessed and validated (Miller, 1995). Gabriella's experiences of her wounded past further echo the impact experienced by Cristina.

> **Gabriella said: *'That place took me back to that fear of, of the world around you in a way... of, of my childhood as well and, and the importance of having, you know, not giving into that whilst looking after yourself. No really, in a very dark area, really.'***

Gabriella's experience is indicative of the therapist's developmental traumas resurfacing within their experience of self-disclosure. Her insistence on ***'not giving in'*** is demonstrative of her robustness and ability to use herself and her self-disclosure as a source of healing for the client and herself. Again, there is a rhythmic resonance that comes through in her repetitive emphasise on words such as **'of'** and **'and',** which conveys the depth of impact and fear that exist in these moments. Gabriella's limbic and rhythmic resonance can also be an attempt to self-soothe (Stern, 1998), as a means of supporting her to talk about and manage the impact this experience may have on her in *this* moment. These experiences of therapist self-disclosure bring to the fore the notion of the therapist as a wounded healer, which is also evident in the following remarks.

> **Jack said: *'Okay, so I'm happy to say I don't flood, I don't tear up. I remind myself why I'm doing it and I tell myself this is for the client, to help the client through that bit. Perhaps it's easier if I give you an example. My brother committed suicide and I had a client going through the same thing and this client thought, imagined, this had***

never happened to anybody else. And I thought, I never thought I'd say this, but I want to tell you something and remind you that you can survive this, you can get through. It won't be easy and I thought I was slightly nervous. I checked with a supervisor and we talked through it. But it, it did something. It certainly lifted something for myself and the client because I would have felt dishonest sitting here not sharing it.'

Jack said: *'I shared with someone who could not see why her husband had just upped and gone. I talked about having being divorced and know what it was like to sit with someone you have loved and divorcing from and I remember my wife, soon to be ex-wife, both in a restaurant and saw my tears falling into a bowl of soup and when I looked across, her tears were falling into a bowl of soup, there were two bowls of soup being filled with tears, and I didn't know whether to laugh or cry and I told this to this poor woman, who was sobbing besides herself when her husband said I'm off and… I think she might have thought that does happen to other people.'*

Jack said: 'There might be some people who go into therapy for a crisis and think it hasn't happened to anyone else, so yeah, that was another disclosure.'

Jack's narrative is an example of his use of his own wounds in the service of healing for his client. By his own admission, in his first remark, he acknowledges feeling anxiety and panic once his self-disclosure was 'out there'. Consequently, he demonstrates self-care by exploring his disclosure in supervision. Interestingly, Jack bravely acknowledges that sometimes within these moments of therapist self-disclosure, when therapists use their wounds in the service of healing, they open themselves up to the possibility of supporting their client to heal and also themselves. Jack's further remark is an illustration of his authentic need to bare his wounds and make transparent his own very personal pain, in the hope of supporting his client to know that she is not alone in her hurt.

Without attempting to take away her pain, he demonstrates that he is there with her, holding his own wounds and using them as a vehicle to help his client work with her own wounds. In this way, his client may use this experience as a platform for transformation and a source of compassion, empathy and strength. Jack's responses provide evidence of the duality that exists in therapist self-disclosure as his narrative powerfully alludes to the notion of the two-way interpersonal process and intersubjective meeting, in which healing in itself is not a one-sided occurrence. This theme of the 'wounded healer' (the duality of the healing for both client and therapist) demonstrates the power of therapist self-disclosure to intimately move both subjectivities and is further supported by Miles' contribution below.

> **Miles said: *'You feel more in tune with the core of who you are, almost the word I want to use is, um... it gets you in touch with your central force of gravity about who you are... I think you're embodying, trying to be authentic and true to yourself, which in my book, for many clients, that's what they're struggling with. As a therapist, being true in certain pockets of time with clients, can help them but I think it can also help the therapist.'***

Miles' experience of disclosing his wounds illustrates the positive impact and healing therapist self-disclosure can have on the therapist, promoting further integration and authenticity within their core self. He goes on to acknowledge that taking the risk of being authentic and true may support clients to also embrace their fear of stepping forward in true self-expression (Winnicott, 1965). Miles' comment reinforces the two-person psychology (Stark, 2000) at play within the therapeutic dyad. By contrast, Anna's comment below takes a different direction in relation to the wounded healer.

> **Anna said: *'You might be sending out a message of, "Here you are, look at me, I've had your experiences but I'm all sorted***

> ***out, I'm a therapist but you're not." The client may be quite narcissistic and not want to know anything about you. They may receive a message of "I've no right to be a victim".'***

Anna's position highlights the ambiguity present in these moments of therapist self-disclosure and reminds us that sometimes, baring our wounds can prove injurious to the client, the work and the therapeutic relationship. Furthermore, when disclosure lands badly, it can also impact the therapist, tearing open old wounds that perhaps have never fully healed. Anna reinforces her point.

> **Anna said: *'My self-esteem's quite tied up in my work, so anything that damages that work, then, er, or threatens that work or impacts that work impacts me, so the thought that I've lost, I may have lost, erm, (pause), that ability, er, now to help him in as much as I could have bothers me.'***

This revelation of a potential rupture in the midst of therapist self-disclosure echoes a strong theme of vulnerability and disempowerment, whilst demonstrating the immense pressure therapists place on themselves in their accountability to be a healing presence for their clients. Her narrative makes transparent self-disclosure's potential to cause emotional injuries and damage to the therapist's self-esteem. I would argue that it also may impact their sense of self as a human being in the world. There is a sense that in these challenging moments, self-doubt manifests, which can also be symbolic of past traumas and wounds being re-ignited.

Considering the two-way interpersonal process that operates throughout the therapeutic relationship, it feels appropriate to reflect on how therapist self-disclosure may impact the disclosing 'wounded healer'. Rowan and Jacobs (2002) state that within this relational dynamic there are moments when self-disclosure serves a dual purpose. This view honours the notion of the two subjectivities, their beings within the therapeutic dyad mutually influencing the other, resulting in transformation and healing for both. Within this relational way of being, both therapist and client are involved in the intrinsic interplay of the shape and feel of the therapeutic relationship, and the shared experience of being-with-self-and-other (DeYoung, 2003). Therapist do acknowledge this dual impact, dual sense of healing that sometimes sharing something of yourself for the client's healing can also heal parts of the therapist.

It feels crucial to acknowledge the impact therapist self-disclosure has on the therapist at multi-levels: emotional, psychological and embodied states. Consequently, it can be argued that holding a conscious awareness of this complex phenomenon operating at multi-levels within both subjectivities (therapist and client) may help therapists to more 'comfortably' own that they too experience healing and/or discomfort in these moments. Often, it is the embodied experience that alerts the therapist that something is happening for them too. I argue that this notion can be extended to therapist self-disclosure, which can also be experienced in an embodied form. It feels appropriate to say that the experience of being wounded emotionally and/or psychologically can support therapists to use their wounds in the service of healing with great empathy and compassion. These moments can also prove emotionally and psychologically injurious for the client (and the therapist) if the shadow side of the therapist delivers the self-disclosure (Storr, 1990).

Consequently, therapists agree that judicious use of self-disclosure, aimed at client benefit, complements and enhances the human dimension. This in turn, strengthens the working alliance, therapeutic relationship and attachment bond between therapist and client, thus allowing movement in the work. The duality of therapist self-disclosure is further reinforced by Storr (1990) and is also evident in the various therapists' accounts detailed in this book, which show that therapists, just like clients, need to feel known, connected, appreciated and respected by the other. What becomes apparent, is the therapists' need for clients to see them as wounded, fallible, imperfect, ordinary and willing participants in the service of healing.

Furthermore, therapists mindfully acknowledge their need as human beings and therapists to have their clients remove them from the pedestal or ivory tower on which clients sometimes place them transferentially. In this sense, what comes through strongly is the therapist's humility - needing clients to see that they too have difficulties, traumas, hurts and wounds, which they continue to work through and manage. It is evident that these very intimate moments require the therapist-client relationship to be secure and sufficiently solidified so that the trust present in these moments remains powerful enough to embrace therapist self-disclosure, transformation and also weather the storm of ruptures.

Chapter 14
Conclusion

Exploring the phenomenon of therapist self-disclosure provides significant insights into the personal experiences and impact on the disclosing therapists themselves and highlights an area that remains under-researched. I integrate in this book existing literature on therapist self-disclosure, which concentrates mainly on the client.

Consequently, it felt important to hold myself accountable in terms of my contribution on this subject matter initiating an attempt to make inroads in relation to bridging an existing gap within the field of counselling psychology and psychotherapy. In this respect, focusing on the impact and personal experience self-revelation has on the disclosing therapist appears apposite. Another aim was to acknowledge the duality operating in the therapeutic dyad in which both subjectivities are open to moments of exposure and vulnerability, both voluntarily and involuntarily, as is the nature of self-disclosure. It felt important to put forward 'the therapist's use of self' and 'the therapist as a wounded healer' as these concepts are integral to forming an appreciation of how self-revelation by the therapist impacts them personally.

Although it is to be expected that therapists maintain a conscious awareness of their experiences during moments of self-disclosure, it must be noted that given the complexity incumbent in human subjectivity, this is not always possible. Nevertheless, it can be argued that such an awareness can enhance both personal and professional development and ensure effective self-care. By fostering a 'felt sense' notion of emotional robustness, consciously working with their shadow parts and continuously building on their reflective capacity, therapists can integrate their imperfections and wounds, thus enriching the therapeutic relationship with humility and humanity.

The personal impact of therapist self-disclosure encompasses emotional, psychological, and embodied dimensions. These extend to the therapist's sense of humanity and their personal emotional traumas and psychological wounds. In recognising this, it becomes evident that therapists need their clients to witness their fallibility and imperfections, which may facilitate a more authentic and healing therapeutic process.

Another area of interest is the importance of *'timing'*, which is underscored in therapist self-disclosure. The notion of a *'right time'* suggests that clients might benefit from early awareness of their therapist's humility and humanity to balance power dynamics and dispel unrealistic expectations. However, therapists must consider client presentations, as those with a strong trauma base or personality disorders may not initially benefit from therapist self-disclosure. These clients may first require developmental processes such as mirroring and idealising before they can engage with the therapist's disclosures.

Moreover, therapist self-disclosure necessitates an acute awareness of subjective and countertransference feelings, personal history, traumas, and challenges. Reflexivity becomes crucial and is key in supporting therapists' personal growth and preventing interference in the client's therapeutic space. Engaging in regular personal therapy, supervision, working with one's shadow and maintaining empathic curiosity may help develop therapists' self-awareness and professional integrity, safeguarding both therapist and client.

Holding the view that self-disclosure is inevitable, it feels important to consider its position in relation to trainee therapists and newly qualified therapists. Regular supervision and personal therapy remain important avenues, as they allow for the possibility to learn about and grapple with therapist self-disclosure and its potential impact. Experience and skill are critical, as inappropriate self-disclosure can be detrimental to both the client and therapist.

Thus, it feels important to encourage training programmes to consider their responsibility to hold a space for this topic and support trainees and newly qualified therapists by offering careful navigation in this area while reminding them of self-disclosure's profound impact - both negative and positive - to client and therapist.

The testimonies in this book have illuminated the profound personal impact of therapist self-disclosure, leading me to advocate increased awareness and integration of this phenomenon within training, supervision and practice. Additionally, it will be important for future research on this phenomenon to continue and to explore the duality of mutual influence between client and therapist, the risks involved, and the ethical considerations as well as the impact on therapist self-care. Disseminating these findings through various channels can facilitate a broader understanding and acceptance of therapist self-disclosure, ultimately enhancing the therapeutic process for all concerned.

Finally, it is very evident that therapists are indeed impacted on a very personal level by the self-disclosures they share with their clients. The most valuable insights in this work are provided by the therapists' personal experiences of their self-disclosures: the transformative impact for the therapist, as well as the vulnerability and anxiety this can elicit at the cost of being relational.

It is hoped that the book will endow readers with knowledge that strengthens arguments in favour of future explorations into the personal impact and experience of therapist self-disclosure on the disclosing therapist. Moreover, the therapists' testimonies highlight the duality of the reciprocal mutual influence for both client and therapist and makes transparent the risk to the therapist in relation to the emotional and psychological impact. Casement (2019, p.83) recognises this duality when he states:

> ***'The patient then needs to find some evidence that this has not only reached the analyst but is having an effect upon him/her. When an analyst is truly in touch with difficult feelings they will be experienced as difficult. Often it is the evidence of emotional contact that counts more than a clever interpretation.'***

In addition, the shared accounts from therapists demonstrate their vulnerability, humanity, 'woundedness' and emotional states that can remain overlooked. In my view, this 'excruciating' cost implies significant 'risk' for the self of the therapist and their self-care. Thus, I postulate that perhaps further attention needs to focus on the areas of therapist self-care in relation to the impact on the disclosing therapist, which may lead to more ethical workings and practice. Continued research in this area may result in reframing perceptions regarding this phenomenon, which in turn may end the disparity that currently exists between ethics and practice.

Immersing myself in this journey has proven transformative in terms of how I position myself in relation to this phenomenon. I am more cognisant of the risks, the impact and the costs, and what it will mean to self-disclose. What has been invaluable in exploring this subject matter is that I now feel a greater resolve to move between safety and risk. I am more confident, equipped and curious to work with therapist self-disclosure. I recognise the importance of fully immersing myself in and wrestling with this phenomenon continuously. Consequently, I am more able, willing and 'comfortable' with sharing more of myself thoughtfully, with intent to aid my client's journey and participate in the service of healing. Moreover, I believe that in sharing more of myself through my self-disclosures, I can acknowledge the duality at play – holding the luminosity and the shadow, and the potential healing for both self-and-other.

Bibliography

Alexander, F. (1961). *The Scope of Psychoanalysis*. New York: Basic Books.

Audet, C.T. (2011). Client Perspectives of Therapist Self-Disclosure: Violating boundaries or removing barriers? *Counselling Psychology Quarterly*, 24 (2), 85-100.

Audet, C. & Everall, R.D. (2003). Counsellor Self-Disclosure: Client-informed implications for practice. *Counselling and Psychotherapy Research*, 3, 223-231.

Baldwin, M. (2000). Interview with Carl Rogers on the use of self in therapy. In M.

Baldwin [Ed.] *The use of self in therapy*. NY: Haworth, pp. 29-38.

Barrett, M. & Berman, J. (2001). Is psychotherapy more effective when therapists disclose information about themselves? Journal of Consulting and Clinical Psychology, 69(4), 597-603.

Bowlby, J. (1998). *A Secure Base*. Oxon: Routledge.

Braud, W. and Anderson, R. (1998). *Transpersonal Research Methods for the social Sciences. Honouring Human Experience*. London: Sage.

Bridges, N.A. (2001). Therapist Self-Disclosure. Expanding the Comfort Zone. *Psychotherapy*, 38, 21-30.

Brown, L.S. & Walker, L.E. (1990). In Stricker, G and Fisher, M. (Eds.), *Self-Disclosure in Therapeutic Relationship*. New York: Plenum, pp.135-157.

Buber, M. (1958) *I and Thou*. New York: Macmillan.

Bugental, J.F. (1987). *The Art of the Psychotherapist*. New York: Norton..

Casement, P. (1985). *On learning from the Patient*. London: Routledge Publication.

Casement, P. (1990). *Further Learning from the Patient. The Analytic Space and Process*. East Sussex. Routledge Publication.

Casement, P. (2019). *Learning Along the Way*. Oxon/New York: Routledge.

Clarkson, P. (1995). *The Therapeutic Relationship*. London: Whurr Publishers Ltd.

DeYoung, P.A. (2003) *Relational Psychotherapy*. New York: Routledge.

Ehrenberg, D.B. (1995). Self-Disclosure: Therapeutic Tool or Indulgence? Countertransference Disclosure. *Contemporary Psychoanalysis.31 (2), 213-228.*

Etherington, K. (2004). *Becoming a Reflexive Researcher, Using Ourselves in Research*. London: Jessica Kingsley Publishers.

Fairbairn, W.R.D. (2010). *Object Relations Theory in the Clinical Setting*. New York: Columbus University Press.

Farber, B.A. (2006). *Self-Disclosure in Psychotherapy*. New York: The Guilford Press.

Ferenczi, S. (1926). *Further Contributions to the Theory and Technique of Psychoanalysis*. Honolulu, HI: Hogarth Press.

Freud, S. (1912). Recommendations to Physicians practicing Psycho-Analysis. *In the standard edition of the Psychological Works of Sigmund Freud*. (Vol.12). London: Hogarth Press, pp1-120.

Gadamer, H.G. (1990). *Truth and Method* (2nd Rev. ed.) (J. Weinsheimer and D.G. Marshall, Trans.). New York: Continuum. (Original work published in 1960).

Bibliography

Gibson, M.F. (2012). Opening Up: Therapist Self-Disclosure in Theory, Research and Practice. *Clinical Social Work Journal*, 40 (3), 287-296.

Goldfried, M.R., Burckell, L.A. & Eubanks-Carter, C. (2003) Therapist Self-Disclosure in Cognitive-Behaviour Therapy. *Journal of Clinical Psychoanalysis/in Session.* 59, 555-568.

Greenspan, M. (1986). *Should Therapists be Personal? Self-Disclosure and Therapeutic Distance in Feminist Therapy.* Women and Therapy, 5, 5-17.

Greenberg, J. (1995). *Self-Disclosure: Is it Psychoanalytic?* Contemporary Psychoanalysis, 31: 193-205.

Guntrip, H.J.S., (1968). *Schizoid Phenomena, Object Relations and the Self.* London: Hogarth Press. *Audet, C. T. (2011). Client perspectives of therapist self-disclosure: Violating boundaries or removing barriers?.* Counselling Psychology Quarterly, 24*(2), 85-100. DOI: 10.1080/09515070.2011.589602*

Hanson, J. (2005). Should your lips be zipped? How therapist self-disclosure and non-disclosure affects clients. *Counselling & Psychotherapy Research*, 5(2), 96-104.

Heidegger, M. (1927) *Being and Time*. Oxford: Blackwell. (1962 text trans J. Macquarrie & E.Robinson).Heidegger, M). New York: Harper. (Original work published 1927).

Hill, J. (1993). *Am I a Kleinian? Is Anyone?* British Journal of Psychotherapy. 9(4):463-75).

Hoffman-Graff, M.A. (1977). Interviewer use of Positive and Negative Self-Disclosure and interviewer subject sex pairing. *Journal of Counselling Psychology*, 25, 517-572.

Jourad, S.M. (1971). *The Transparent Self. (2nd.ed.).* New York: Van Nostrand.

Jung, C.G. (1993). *The Basic Writings of C.G. Jung*. New York: Random House Publishing.

Kaiser, T. (1997). *Supervisory Relationships: Exploring the Human Element.* Pacific Grove, CA: Brooks Cole.

Khan, M. (1986). Outrageousness, Compliance and Authenticity. *Contemporary Psychoanalysis*, 22, 629-652.

Knox, S., Hess, S. A., Petersen, D. A. & Hill, C. E. (1997). A Qualitative Analysis of Client Perceptions of the Effects of Helpful Therapist Self-Disclosure in Long-term Therapy. *Journal of Counselling Psychology*, 44, 274–283.

Knox, S. & Hill, C. E. (2003). Therapist Self-Disclosure: Research-based suggestions for Practitioners. *Journal of Clinical Psychology*, 59, 529 – 539.

Kohut, H. (1971). *The Analysis of the Self.* New York: International Universities Press.

Lane, R.C. & Hull, J.W. (1990). Self-Disclosure and Classical Psychoanalysis. In G. Stricker and M. Fishe (Eds.). Self-Disclosure in the Therapeutic Relationship. New York: Plenuim Press, pp.31-46.

Lapworth, P., Sills, C. & Fish, S. (2001). *Integration in Couselling and Psychotherapy. Developing a Personal Approach.* London: Sage.

Mahalik J.R, Van Ormer, E.A. & Simi, N.L. (2000) Ethical Issues in using Self-Disclosure in Feminist Therapy. In Brabeck M.M. (Ed.), *Practising Feminist Ethics in Psychology* Washington, DC: American Psychological Association, pp.189-201).

Marais, G. and McBeath A.G. (2021). *Therapists Lived Experience of Therapist self-Disclosure.* European Journal of Qualitative Research. Vol.11, 72-86.

Maroda, K. (1991). *The Power of Countertransference*. New York: John Wiley.

McBeath A. G. (2019). The Motivations of Psychotherapists: An in-depth survey. Counselling and Psychotherapy Research, 19(4), 377–387.

Mearns, D & Cooper M, (2005). *Working at Relational Depth in Psychotherapy.* Thousand Oaks: Sage Publications Inc.

Bibliography

Miller, A. (1995). *The Drama of being a Child: The Search for the True Self.* London: The Little Brown Book Group.

Miller, G.D. & Baldwin, D.C. (2000). *Implications of the Wounded-Healer Paradigm for the Use of Self in Therapy,* in M Baldwin (ed.) *The Use of Self in Therapy,* (2nd ed.). Binghamton NY: Hayworth Press, pp.243-261.

Myers, D. & Hayes, J. A. (2006). Effects of Therapist general Self-disclosure and Countertransference Disclosure on ratings of the Therapist and Session. *Psychotherapy: Theory, Research, Practice, Training,* 43, (2), 173–185.

Orange, D., Atwood, G. & Stolorow, R. (1997), *Working Intersubjectively: Contextualism in Psychoanalytic Practice.* Hillsdale, NJ: The Analytic Press.

Peterson, Z.D (2002). More than a Mirror: The Ethics of Self-Disclosure. *Psychotherapy: Theory, Research, Practice, Training,* 39 (1), 21-31.

Pizer, B. (1993). *When the analyst is ill: Dimensions of Self-Disclosure.* Psychoanalytic Quarterly, 64, 466-495.

Renik, O. (1995). *The Ideal of the Anonymous Analyst and the Problem of Self-Disclosure,* Psychoanalytic Quarterly, 64: 466-95.

Rogers, C. (1951). *On Becoming a Person.* Boston: Houghton Mifflin.

Rogers, C. R. (1961). *On Becoming a Person: A therapist's View of Psychotherapy.* London: Constable.

Rothschild, B. (2003). *The Body Remembers: Casebook. Unifying Methods and Models in the Treatment of Trauma and PTSD.* New York: W.W. Norton & Company, Inc.

Rowan, J. & Jacobs, M. (2002). *The Therapist's Use of Self.* Berkshire: Open University Press.

Safran, J. & Muran, J.C. (2000). *Negotiating the Therapeutic Alliance: A Relational Treatment Guide.* New York: Guilford Press.

Samuels, A. (1985). *Jung and the Post-Jungians.* London: Routledge & Kegan Paul.

Schore, A.N. (2005). Attachment, Affect Regulation, and the Developing Right Brain: linking Developmental Neuroscience to Paediatrics. *Paediatrics in Review,* 26, 204-211.

Siegel, D.J. (1999). *The Developing Mind.* New York: the Guildford Press.

Simon, J.C (1990). *Criteria for Therapist Self-Disclosure.* In Stricker, G. and Fisher, M. (Eds.), *Self-Disclosure in the Therapeutic Relationship.* New York, NY: Plenum, pp. 207-225.

Smith, J.A, Flowers, P & Larkin, M. (2009). *Interpretative Phenomenological Analysis: Theory, Method and Research. London:* Sage Publications.

Spinelli, E. (2002). *The Mirror and the Hammer: Challenges to Therapeutic Orthodoxy.* London: Sage.

Spinelli, E. (2005). *The Interpreted World: An Introduction to Phenomenological Psychology* (2nd ed.). London: SAGE.

Stark, M. (2000). Modes of Therapeutic Action. New Jersey: Jason Aronson.

Stern, D. (1998). *The Interpersonal World of the Infant: A View from Psychoanalysis and Developmental Psychology.* London: Karnac Ltd.

Stolorow, R.D., Brandchaft, B. & Atwood G.E. (1987) *Psychoanalytic Treatment: An Intersubjective Approach. Psychoanalytic Inquiry Book Series.* Vol.8. Hillsdale NJ: The Analytic Press.

Storr, A. (1990). *The Art of Psychotherapy* (2nd ed.). Oxford: Butterworth-Heinemann.

Sullivan, H.S. (1954). *The Psychiatric Interview.* New York: W.W. Norton and Co.

Sweezey, M. (2005). Not Confidential: Therapist Considerations in Self-Disclosure. *Smith*

College Studies in Social Work, 75 (1), 81-91.

Tantillo, M.M. (2004). *The Therapist's use of Self-Disclosure in a Relational Therapy Approach for Eating Disorders. Eating Disorders*, 12 (1), 51-73.

Wachtel, P. (2008). *Relational Theory and the Practice of Psychotherapy*. New York: London: The Guilford Press.

Watkins, C.E. (1990). The Effects of Counsellor Self-Disclosure: A Research Review. *The Counselling Psychologist,* 18, 477-500.

Wells, T.L. (1994). Therapist Self-Disclosure: Its effects on Clients and the Treatment Relationship. *Smith College Studies in Social Work, 65, 23-41.*

Winnicott, D. (1965). *The Maturational Process and the Facilitating Environment.* London: Hogarth Press.

Yalom, I.D. (2002). *The Gift of Therapy: Reflections on Being a Therapist.* London: Piatkus Books.

Zahm, S. (1998). Therapist Self-Disclosure in the Practice of Gestalt Therapy, *The Gestalt Journal*, 21 (2): 21-52.

Zur, O. & Lazarus, A.A. (2002). *Dual Relationships in Psychotherapy. New York: Springer.*

Zur, O. (2009). Therapeutic Boundaries and Effective Therapy. In O'Donohue, W. and Graybar, S.R. (Eds.). *Handbook of Contemporary Psychotherapy: Toward an improved understanding of Effective Psychotherapy.* Thousand Oaks: Sage Publications Inc, pp. 341-357.

www.ingramcontent.com/pod-product-compliance
Lightning Source LLC
LaVergne TN
LVHW050917210926
848482LV00012B/471
9781036906627